MODERNIZING
THE STRATEGIC BOMBER FORCE

Studies in Defense Policy
TITLES PUBLISHED

Naval Force Levels and Modernization:
An Analysis of Shipbuilding Requirements
Arnold M. Kuzmack

Support Costs in the Defense Budget: The Submerged One-Third
Martin Binkin

The Changing Soviet Navy
Barry M. Blechman

Strategic Forces: Issues for the Mid-Seventies
Alton H. Quanbeck and Barry M. Blechman

U.S. Reserve Forces: The Problem of the Weekend Warrior
Martin Binkin

U.S. Force Structure in NATO: An Alternative
Richard D. Lawrence and Jeffrey Record

U.S. Tactical Air Power: Missions, Forces, and Costs
William D. White

U.S. Nuclear Weapons in Europe: Issues and Alternatives
Jeffrey Record with the assistance of Thomas I. Anderson

The Control of Naval Armaments: Prospects and Possibilities
Barry M. Blechman

Stresses in U.S.-Japanese Security Relations
Fred Greene

The Military Pay Muddle
Martin Binkin

Sizing Up the Soviet Army
Jeffrey Record

Modernizing the Strategic Bomber Force: Why and How
Alton H. Quanbeck and Archie L. Wood
with the assistance of Louisa Thoron

ALTON H. QUANBECK *and* ARCHIE L. WOOD
with the assistance of Louisa Thoron

MODERNIZING
THE STRATEGIC BOMBER FORCE
Why and How

THE BROOKINGS INSTITUTION
Washington, D.C.

Copyright © 1976 by
THE BROOKINGS INSTITUTION
1775 Massachusetts Avenue, N.W., Washington, D.C. 20036

Library of Congress Cataloging in Publication Data:
Quanbeck, Alton H 1926–
  Modernizing the strategic bomber force.
  (Studies in defense policy)
  1. Bombers. 2. United States—Air defenses,
Military. 3. B-1 bomber. I. Wood, Archie L., joint
author. II. Thoron, Louisa, joint author. III. Title.
IV. Series.
UG1242.B6Q36   358.4′2   75-38890
ISBN 0-8157-7281-5

9 8 7 6 5 4 3 2 1

THE BROOKINGS INSTITUTION is an independent organization devoted to nonpartisan research, education, and publication in economics, goevernment, foreign policy, and the social sciences generally. Its principal purposes are to aid in the development of sound public policies and to promote public understanding of issues of national importance.

The Institution was founded on December 8, 1927, to merge the activities of the Institute for Government Research, founded in 1916, the Institute of Economics, founded in 1922, and the Robert Brookings Graduate School of Economics and Government, founded in 1924.

The Board of Trustees is responsible for the general administration of the Institution, while the immediate direction of the policies, program, and staff is vested in the President, assisted by an advisory committee of the officers and staff. The bylaws of the Institution state: "It is the function of the Trustees to make possible the conduct of scientific research, and publication, under the most favorable conditions, and to safeguard the independence of the research staff in the pursuit of their studies and in the publication of the results of such studies. It is not a part of their function to determine, control, or influence the conduct of particular investigations or the conclusions reached."

The President bears final responsibility for the decision to publish a manuscript as a Brookings book. In reaching his judgment on the competence, accuracy, and objectivity of each study, the President is advised by the director of the appropriate research program and weighs the views of a panel of expert outside readers who report to him in confidence on the quality of the work. Publication of a work signifies that it is deemed a competent treatment worthy of public consideration but does not imply endorsement of conclusions or recommendations.

The Institution maintains its position of neutrality on issues of public policy in order to safeguard the intellectual freedom of the staff. Hence interpretations or conclusions in Brookings publications should be understood to be solely those of the authors and should not be attributed to the Institution, to its trustees, officers, or other staff members, or to the organizations that support its research.

FOREWORD

As part of its strategic offensive arsenal, the United States maintains a large bomber force at an annual cost of $6 billion. This cost accounts for about 35 percent of all expenditures on strategic forces. At present a new strategic bomber, the B-1, is being developed, and when Congress considers the budget for fiscal year 1977, it will be asked to decide whether the United States should produce the B-1. Considerable controversy surrounds this impending decision, since the new bomber is likely to be the most expensive weapon system yet developed. Current cost estimates are running over $20 billion, exclusive of armament for the aircraft and operating and support costs.

The controversy over the B-1 has raised many questions about the strategic bomber force as a whole, and some critics contend that bombers are obsolete in an age of missiles. This study addresses these questions in the broadest possible terms, going beyond the usual boundaries of comparative analyses of competing weapons in its review of the historical origins of the bomber force, the justifications advanced for retaining the force, the role of bombers in relation to other strategic offensive forces, the policies that have the greatest effect on setting the task of the bomber force, and arms control possibilities that could both help and hinder the force in the future.

After assessing the current Air Force bomber program, the authors present a comparative cost-effectiveness analysis of representative bomber force alternatives and a bomber force made up of B-1s. In their conclusions and recommendations, they stress the primary purpose of the bomber force as that of ensuring against the failure of the retaliatory capability of the U.S. missile force. This purpose, they believe, can be fulfilled for some time to come by the present strategic bomber force and ultimately by a less costly weapon system than the B-1. It is their hope that their analyses will help to focus and inform the debate on this important issue and will be of aid to those who must decide on the right course of action for modernizing the bomber force.

Alton H. Quanbeck, Archie L. Wood, and Louisa Thoron were members of the defense analysis staff of the Brookings Foreign Policy Studies program when this study was written. Quanbeck served as its director from 1971 to 1975, Wood was a senior fellow, and Thoron was a research assistant.

The Brookings Institution acknowledges the assistance of the Ford Foundation, which provided a grant in support of the institution's defense and foreign policy studies. It further wishes to thank Philip Odeen, Charles Rossotti, Andrew Borden, and Richard Garwin for their helpful comments on the study.

The authors are indebted to Joseph A. Yager for his review of the manuscript, to Tadd Fisher for her editorial assistance, and to Ann Ziegler who typed the manuscript.

The views expressed are those of the authors and should not be attributed to the Ford Foundation or to the trustees, officers, or other staff members of the Brookings Institution.

KERMIT GORDON
President

December 1975
Washington, D.C.

CONTENTS

1. **Introduction**   1

2. **Is a Strategic Bomber Force Needed?**   4
The Mission of U.S. Strategic Nuclear Forces *4*
Secondary Considerations in Assessing the Need for Bombers *12*
How Big a Task Should the Bomber Force be Designed to Do? *19*
Is Modernizing the Strategic Bomber Force Urgent? *20*
Summary *21*

3. **The Present Course**   23
Systems and Costs *24*
The Projected Program and Its Costs *35*

4. **Bomber Prelaunch Survivability**   39
Airborne Alert *40*
Ground Alert and the SLBM Threat *41*
Bomber Force Variables *46*
Survivability Propects for Bombers on Ground Alert *51*
Tanker Survivability *55*
The Threat of Submarine-Launched Cruise Missiles *57*
Arms Control Considerations and Bomber Prelaunch Survivability *58*
Summary *60*

5. **Penetration of Enemy Air Defenses**   63
Soviet Air Defenses *63*
Is There an Air Defense Penetration Problem? *66*
Projected Soviet Developments and Possible U.S. Reactions *72*
Arms Control Considerations *82*
Summary *83*

6. **Analysis of Alternative Forces**   85
The Military Task *85*
Analytical Results *88*
Possible Evolution of Threats and Forces *91*

7. **Conclusions and Recommendations**   93
Need for a Bomber Force *94*
Present Program *94*
Prelaunch Survivability *95*
Penetration *96*
Alternative Forces *97*
Arms Control Measures *97*

Appendixes
A. Cost Methodology and Projections *99*
B. The Mathematics of Prelaunch Survivability (Ground Alert) *108*
C. Air Defense Penetration Calculations *112*

Tables
2-1. Possible U.S. Forces under the Vladivostok Guidelines   11

3-1. U.S. Bomber and Tanker Force, Selected Fiscal Years   24

3-2. B-1 Cost Estimates for Selected Years   29

3-3. Projected Number of Bombers, Tankers, and Air-to-Surface
Missiles, Fiscal Years 1976–85   36

3-4. Projected Costs of the Bomber and Tanker Program,
Fiscal Years 1976–85   37

4-1. Estimated Number of Soviet SLBMs That Could be
Kept on Station, Depending on Submarine Transit Speed
and Size of Crew   43

4-2. Bomber Reaction-Time Budgets for Crisis and
Day-to-Day Alerts   47

5-1. Unmodified B-52s Required to Deliver 1,200 SRAMs
to Targets against Area Defenses of Different Effectiveness   75

5-2. Modified B-52s or B-1s Required to Deliver 1,200 SRAMs
to Targets against Area Defenses of Different Effectiveness   76

5-3. Missile Carriers Required to Deliver 1,200 ALCMs against
Area Defenses of Different Effectiveness   76

5-4. Number of SAM Sites That Would Have to Be Destroyed
to Give Cruise Missiles Unimpeded Access to the
50 Largest Soviet Cities   78

6-1. Alternative Forces Designed for Approximately Equal
Effectiveness against Threat Level 1   88

6-2. Estimated Performance of the Five Alternative Bomber
Forces against Threat Level 1   89

6-3. Estimated Ten-Year Costs of the Five Alternative Bomber
Forces and Annual Operating Costs in 1985   90

6-4. Comparison of the Capability of the Five Alternative
Bomber Forces to Deliver Missiles against
Threat Levels 2, 3, and 4   91

A-1. Estimated Procurement Costs for the B-1 Bomber, 1976–83   99

A-2. Estimated Costs of Various Bomber Force Components   100

A-3. Annual Operating Costs of the Bomber Force on
40 Percent Alert and 60 Percent Alert   101

A-4. Projected Systems and Costs, Force 1, Fiscal Years 1976–85   102

A-5. Projected Systems and Costs, Force 2, Fiscal Years 1976–85   103

A-6. Projected Systems and Costs, Force 3, Fiscal Years 1976–85   104

A-7. Projected Systems and Costs, Force 4, Fiscal Years 1976–85   105

A-8. Projected Systems and Costs, Force 5, Fiscal Years 1976–85   106

B-1. Lethal Radii against Targets of Varying Hardness for
1- and 2-Megaton Warheads   109

C-1. Fifty Largest Soviet Cities, Their Populations, and the
Radius of the Circle Enclosing 95 Percent of the
Built-up Area of Each City   115

Figures

4-1. Distance Flown by Fast Hard, Soft High-Acceleration,
and Slow Soft Aircraft As a Function of Time
after Brake Release   48

4-2. Survival Probability for Fast Hard, Soft High-Acceleration,
and Slow Soft Aircraft Dispersed on 75 Bases and
Attacked by 300 1-Megaton SLBMs   52

4-3. Effects of Hardness on the Survivability of Fast Hard
Aircraft Dispersed on 75 Bases and Attacked by 300
1-Megaton SLBMs Flying Depressed Trajectories   53

4-4. Effects of Dispersal and Hardness on the Survivability
of Fast Hard Aircraft Attacked by 300 1-Megaton
SLBMs Flying Depressed Trajectories   54

4-5. Effects of Dispersal on the Survivability of the Three
Aircraft Types Attacked by 300 and by 500 SLBMs
Flying Depressed Trajectories   55

4-6. Survival Probabilities versus Reaction Time for the Three
Aircraft Types with Different Dispersal Levels, Attacked
by 300 1-Megaton Depressed Trajectory SLBMs   56

B-1. Bomber Survival Probability versus the Ratio of
Lethal Radius to the Radius of Uncertainty for Various
Levels of Attack   111

CHAPTER ONE

INTRODUCTION

Uniquely, strategic bombers and strategic bombardment continue to play a major role in the contemporary American military posture. Although other nations have built and employed such weapons, none have lavished as much energy and wealth on their development as the United States has. The United States first developed a sizable strategic bombing force during World War II and emerged from the war with nuclear weapons for which bombers were the only means of delivery.

During the postwar period the United States developed the B-36, B-47, B-52, and B-58 bomber aircraft and in the late 1950s initiated the development of the B-70, a high-altitude supersonic heavy bomber, but terminated the program after two test vehicles were built. A program to build about 200 FB-111s—a smaller bomber—was begun in the mid-sixties; this, too, however, was stopped after about 75 were actually deployed. Of all these planes the B-52s were the most capable and versatile, particularly the G and H models. The last of these models were delivered in the early sixties, but they were updated and modernized throughout that decade and are still being improved. They are now the backbone of the strategic bomber force.

The United States applies about 35 percent of all money spent on its strategic forces to bombers. About 25 percent of the nuclear weapons in the strategic arsenal are carried by bombers, and the B-52G/Hs could carry many more. There are now no serious threats to the effectiveness of the B-52 force. Defense Department officials believe that the bomber force could survive a surprise attack by Soviet offensive forces and penetrate Soviet air defenses. Nonetheless, the United States is now on the threshold of a program to modernize the bomber force. The centerpiece of this program is the B-1, which will enter the operational force in the 1980s if present plans are carried out. Current official estimates of the investment cost

1

of the B-1 force now total more than $80 million per airplane, if 244 are produced as proposed by the Air Force.

The forerunner of the B-1, the advanced manned strategic aircraft (AMSA), was conceived soon after the demise of the B-70 program. From its inception, the AMSA was controversial. The Air Force advocated the initiation of the program throughout the late 1960s, but effort was limited to the advance development of components of the AMSA and to system studies of the AMSA weapon system. Soon after the change of administration in 1969, however, the AMSA was redesignated the B-1 and the development of prototypes began.

Some analysts have challenged the need for strategic bombers in an age of ballistic missiles carrying thousands of warheads; others have acknowledged the need for strategic bombers but not for a new bomber at this time; and still others have questioned the characteristics being designed into the B-1, especially its supersonic flight capabilities. Critics have argued as well that a new approach to strategic bombers—the so-called standoff bomber, which would launch missiles against its targets from outside defense perimeters—should be employed in modernizing the strategic bomber force. They have also stressed the costs of the B-1, arguing implicitly or explicitly that it is not worth the money.

Since the B-1 was first conceived, advances in propulsion systems, guidance systems, and the design of ballistic missiles have made alternative approaches to the modernization of the bomber force technologically feasible. Moreover, the treaty limiting the deployment of antiballistic missiles (ABMs)[1] has provided political assurances that an effective ABM defense will not be deployed, and economic and technological impediments to an effective ABM defense are likely to persist. The United States will soon have more than 7,000 ballistic missile reentry vehicles deployed that could defeat any but the most massively deployed and extremely sophisticated ABM system. About 5,000 of these reentry vehicles will be based in nuclear-powered ballistic missile submarines (SSBNs), the most survivable deployment mode the United States has. The other 2,000 will be carried by intercontinental ballistic missiles (ICBMs). Both the submarine-launched ballistic missile force and the land-based ICBM force are capable of surviving a surprise attack. The penetration capabilities of both forces are protected by the ABM treaty. Moreover, the use of only a small

1. Treaty between the United States of America and the Union of Soviet Socialist Republics on the Limitation of Anti-Ballistic Missile Systems, signed at Moscow, May 26, 1972.

fraction of the ballistic missile reentry vehicles could destroy major elements of Soviet air defenses and would disrupt the operation of the system as a whole. Thus the ABM treaty gives added assurance, too, of bomber penetration.[2]

The purpose of this study is to explore key issues relating to the modernization of the bomber force. Does the United States need a bomber force? If so, is its modernization urgent? What approaches, other than the B-1, are available to modernize the bomber force? Which of these are most economically efficient? What risks for the United States does each involve?

We consider five alternative bomber forces:

—Modified B-52G/Hs (including rocket assistance for faster takeoff).

—B-1s.

—A derivative of large transport aircraft, such as the C-5 or the Boeing 747.

—New aircraft designed for maximum ability to survive a surprise attack.

—A derivative of large transport aircraft with rocket assistance for faster takeoff.

The first two of these forces would be armed with decoys and short-range attack missiles; the other three would carry long-range ballistic or cruise missiles.

We evaluate the five alternative forces and compare their costs, ability to survive a surprise attack (prelaunch survivability), and ability to penetrate Soviet defenses. In our discussion of the problems of prelaunch survivability and the penetration of enemy defenses, we have assumed that the Soviet Union will eventually possess greater capabilities than it has at the present time. Finally, we conclude the study with a presentation of our views on how the bomber force should be modernized.

2. The Soviet Union currently possesses more ballistic missiles than the United States plans to deploy. These missiles are larger than those of the United States as well, but the USSR is only beginning to deploy multiple independently targetable reentry vehicles on their missiles. (The United States began such deployments about five years ago.) Most Soviet missiles, too, would survive a first strike. In effect, since both Soviet and American ABMs are limited by the ABM treaty to 100 interceptors, both superpowers would be devastated should an all-out nuclear war occur.

CHAPTER TWO

IS A STRATEGIC BOMBER FORCE NEEDED?

Among the arguments advanced for and against the retention and modernization of the bomber force, one heard frequently is that bombers are unnecessary in an age of ballistic missiles. The question posed in the title of this chapter cannot be so summarily dismissed, however, for the matter is not that simple. The mission of the strategic forces of the United States is both political and military in nature. The components of these forces—intercontinental ballistic missiles (ICBMs), submarine-launched ballistic missiles (SLBMs), and bombers—interact with one another and with U.S. tactical nuclear and conventional forces in deterring wars and, if deterrence fails, in fighting wars. Thus the need for a bomber force can best be determined by examining the contributions of bombers to the defense of the United States in the context of the overall objectives of the strategic forces.

The Mission of U.S. Strategic Nuclear Forces

The United States acquires and maintains nuclear forces for four principal reasons:
    —To deter nuclear attacks on the United States.
    —To help deter conventional and nuclear attacks on U.S. allies.
    —To strengthen U.S. power and influence in world affairs.
    —To engage in nuclear wars should deterrence fail.
    The first of these objectives has enjoyed the highest priority in planning U.S. strategic nuclear forces. It is widely believed that the best way to meet this objective is to maintain powerful retaliatory forces capable of inflicting so-called unacceptable destruction on any nation that launches a nuclear attack against the United States.

In carrying out the second objective, conventional forces are of primary importance, but the United States backs up these forces to deter attacks on its allies with tactical and strategic nuclear weapons. Were deterrence to fail and the United States and its allies to face the catastrophic defeat of their conventional forces, the threat of using nuclear weapons might deter the adversary from exploiting his military advantages, and the actual use of such weapons might avert the impending defeat of conventional forces. But to pursue either course of action might result in the escalation of the conflict to higher levels of nuclear violence. This risk reduces the credibility of threats to use nuclear forces, especially when there is no nuclear provocation. Some officials, however, believe that the risk of escalation can be reduced by limiting nuclear attacks in scale, geography, or purpose and that forces capable of such limited attacks enhance the effectiveness of U.S. conventional and nuclear forces in deterring attacks on U.S. allies.

The third objective is based on the recognition that nuclear forces contribute to the political image of nations. The fact that the United States and the Soviet Union possess nuclear arsenals that are larger and more varied by far than those of other powers is an important reason for their superpower status. Since the late 1960s when the Soviet Union gained numerical parity with the United States in nuclear forces, many government leaders have been stressing that U.S. strategic nuclear offensive forces must continue to be perceived abroad as at least equal to those of the Soviet Union. They maintain that this perception of "essential equivalence" is important to the nation's image, arguing that it increases the confidence of allies and other friendly countries in the United States and reinforces the impression that adversaries have of U.S. strength and determination.[1]

But the concept of essential equivalence is a complex one. For example, judging the extent to which U.S. and Soviet strategic forces are essentially equivalent requires balancing U.S. advantages in bombers, missile accuracy, and missile warheads against the USSR's larger and more numer-

1. The growing sensitivity to the political aspects of nuclear forces was reflected in the report of the secretary of defense on his budget for fiscal year 1976. For the first time, he presented the need for essential equivalence before discussing the need for an assured retaliatory capability, suggesting a revised set of priorities in the acquisition of nuclear forces. See "Report of Secretary of Defense James R. Schlesinger to the Congress on the FY 1976 and Transition Budgets, FY 1977 Authorization Request and FY 1976–1980 Defense Programs" (February 5, 1975; processed), p. I-13.

ous missiles. Furthermore, since this judgment for the most part pertains to the political consequences of force imbalances rather than to military ones, it is qualitative and subjective. U.S. and Soviet strategic offensive and defensive forces are asymmetric in many ways, and major geographical, geopolitical, and technological asymmetries have important implications for the strategic balance. Therefore it is impossible to be precise about how essential equivalence bears on U.S. force requirements.

The fourth objective—maintaining nuclear forces for fighting a nuclear war—has not in fact determined the size of U.S. strategic forces. U.S. policy has been to prevent nuclear war; therefore emphasis has been placed on the first two objectives and more recently on the third. Former Secretary of Defense James Schlesinger went to great lengths to point out that the size of U.S. strategic offensive forces does not depend on warfighting criteria but on the size of Soviet forces—that is, on maintaining essential equivalence. Previous secretaries of defense have cited deterrence requirements to justify the size of U.S. strategic forces.

The Bomber's Role in Deterrence

Bombers were once the backbone of U.S. deterrent forces, but that role has been taken over by the other strategic forces, the ICBMs and SLBMs. Nonetheless, today bombers serve as insurance against the failure of the missile forces, as Secretary Schlesinger emphasized in his budget report to Congress in 1975.

The most tried and tested of our strategic retaliatory forces—the heavy bombers—continue to interact with our ICBMs to heighten the survivability of both. *At the same time, they provide us with a hedge against failure in our other retaliatory capabilities.*[2] (Emphasis added.)

Some strategists believe that the survivability of fixed ICBMs, and therefore their retaliatory potential, will decline from the present high level sometime within the next decade.[3] Partly in anticipation of such an even-

2. Ibid., p. I-15.
3. This view is by no means unanimous. Many experts doubt that an attack sufficiently well-coordinated to overcome "fratricide" effects (the destruction of some attacking missiles by others) can be carried out. Some are skeptical about whether the generation of Soviet missiles now being deployed are sufficiently accurate to destroy nearly all the U.S. ICBM force. Still other strategists suggest that U.S. ICBMs could be launched even after weapons have begun exploding over American bomber bases. If these views are correct, the cases for the deployment of both the B-1 and Trident are weakened.

tuality, the United States is engaged in developing and deploying the Trident weapon system, a submarine-based ICBM. The announced force goal of ten Trident submarines armed with Trident I missiles will have about the same retaliatory capability as 200 Minuteman IIIs. (Many analysts believe that about 300 surviving Minuteman IIIs would constitute an acceptable retaliatory capability.) The advent of the Trident II, an even larger and more powerful missile than the Trident I, might double the retaliatory capability of the Trident submarines.[4]

Barring the most dramatic sort of antisubmarine warfare (ASW) breakthrough, U.S. strategic ballistic missile submarines (SSBNs) armed with nuclear missiles are likely to remain highly survivable. The problems associated with the development of an effective ASW threat to SSBNs appear to be nearly insoluble for the Soviet Union because of its limited access to the sea and its remoteness from waters in which the United States can easily and routinely operate its SSBNs. Furthermore, U.S. marine technology is superior to that of the Soviet Union. Even more implausible than the prospect of ASW threats is that they could materialize suddenly without the necessary development and testing activities being detected well in advance of deployment. As a consequence, the United States would have time to implement a host of countermeasures, just as it has when other real and potential threats, such as air defenses, have occurred. Even so, ASW breakthroughs cannot be totally ruled out. Thus such possibilities constitute one of the justifications for retaining a bomber force.

In addition, there are questions about the survivability of communications to SSBNs. These are often raised to cast doubt on the desirability of putting more retaliatory capability in submarines. The emphasis placed by Secretary Schlesinger on the potential of the SLBMs as the withholdable reserve (that is, the strategic nuclear force that could be held back after an initial nuclear exchange), implied that communications to the SLBMs have adequate survivability. On the other hand, he argued that communications to the submarines are less survivable than the submarines themselves.[5]

In an effort to improve communications to SSBNs, the Department of Defense has proposed the deployment of an extremely low-frequency (ELF) transmitting system, called Sanguine, that would use many under-

4. Congressman Robert L. Leggett of California gave estimated Trident payloads in "Two Legs Do Not a Centipede Make," *Armed Forces Journal International,* vol. 112 (February 1975), p. 30.
5. See "Report on the FY 1976 and Transition Budgets," p. II-53.

ground hardened antennas spread over a large area. Advanced satellite communication systems might also have some future application.

As Trident I and Trident II become operational, communications could be improved further. New tactical possibilities would be afforded to both the submarines and the existing airborne communications relays because the longer range of the Trident missiles would permit U.S. submarines to operate in wider areas that are remote from the USSR. Thus, for example, the risk of having the submarine antennas detected would be reduced and ELF communications with SSBNs operating close to the United States would be facilitated.

While it is probably safe to assume that communications to U.S. SSBNs are now adequate and will remain so as long as the United States stays alert for problems and pursues solutions aggressively when they arise, the remaining uncertainty, though small, is another argument for continuing to retain a competent strategic bomber force. The prospect of increased reliance on U.S. sea-based retaliatory forces as land-based missiles become more vulnerable reinforces this line of reasoning.

The second element of deterrence—the capability of nuclear weapons to reinforce the deterrent to attacks on U.S. allies—presupposes a nuclear force adequate to deter attacks on the United States and a capability for limited nuclear attacks that can be linked to conventional warfare. The limited-attack capability can best be provided by tactical nuclear forces —fighter-bombers (F-111s, F-4s), carrier-based aircraft, nuclear artillery, short- and medium-range missiles (Lance, Pershing)—and ICBMs. As Secretary Schlesinger pointed out:

The ICBM force, the heart of which is the Minuteman series, continues to give us the accuracy, flexibility, and control necessary to deal with and thereby deter a wide range of attacks on military targets. *It provides the most reliable source of limited response options so essential to nuclear deterrence under conditions of parity.*[6] (Emphasis added.)

Fighter-bombers and carrier-based aircraft must be retained in any event for conventional war, and they are faster and have better penetration capabilities than strategic bombers. Tactical and strategic ballistic missiles are extremely fast and virtually invulnerable to enemy air defenses.

In sum, the United States has anticipated the prospective diminution of fixed ICBM survivability by initiating the Trident program and will continue to rely primarily on tactical nuclear systems and ICBMs for limited nuclear attack capabilities. Thus, while reliance on the bomber

6. Ibid., p. I-14.

force as a deterrent is not increasing perceptibly, there is some justification for retaining bombers as a hedge against the failure of other retaliatory capabilities.

The Bomber's Role in Maintaining Essential Equivalence

Until about 1969 U.S. strategic forces surpassed those of the Soviet Union in almost every index of strategic power. Now Soviet missile forces are numerically larger and carry more payload, or throw-weight, although the Soviet bomber force is smaller and its aircraft are older and less capable than those of the U.S. force.[7] The Soviet Union has also begun to deploy missiles carrying multiple independently targetable reentry vehicles (MIRVs), which could lead to Soviet numerical superiority in deployed warheads as well, even within the equal ceilings on missiles with MIRVs called for in the Vladivostok guidelines.[8] Thus if maintaining essential equivalence is to be an important objective in the management of U.S. strategic offensive forces, keeping up with Soviet force deployments may

7. The Soviet Union, which had no strategic bombardment legacy from the Second World War, has pursued a different course from that of the United States in the development of its strategic offensive forces, giving greatest emphasis to land-based strategic missiles. Soviet military leaders spelled out their rationale for de-emphasizing strategic bombers as follows:

"Today, the [Soviet] Air Force is in a special situation. In recent years, there has been keen competition between the bomber, the missile, and air defense weapons. In this competition, air defense weapons have gained a great advantage over bomber aviation. Long-range bombers . . . whose flight it is practically impossible to conceal, given the modern radar reconnaissance resources, have become especially vulnerable. In covering great distances at relatively low flight speeds, long-range bombers will often be forced to be in an air defense zone for extended periods of time, which seriously complicates their carrying out combat operations.

"Consequently, the missions of destruction of targets deep in the enemy's territory will be executed more reliably by the Strategic Rocket Troops.

"True, 'air-to-ground' type missiles with range up to 400–600 kilometers and more have been developed on a broad scale abroad. This is considerably expanding the capacities of long-range bombers which are beginning to be converted into rocket carriers capable of delivering blows at enemy targets without entering the zone of his air defense. Thus, for example, the *Hound Dog* missile (range of about 800 kilometers) has been incorporated into the U.S. strategic air force's arsenal; and in England the *Blue Steel* missile (range: 600–1,000 kilometers) is being developed. *But even in this case the strategic bomber aircraft cannot regain its lost importance.* [Emphasis added.] Its speed is too low as compared with that of ballistic missiles." (V. D. Sokolovsky, ed., Harriet Fast Scott, trans., *Soviet Military Strategy,* 3d ed. [Moscow: Military Publishing House, 1968], pp. 260–61.)

8. Joint Soviet-American Statement on Strategic Arms Limitation, November 24, 1974.

become a dominant factor in setting upper limits on the overall size of U.S. strategic forces.

Current perceptions of the contributions of U.S. bombers to the maintenance of essential equivalence are ambiguous. Some administration spokesmen have expressed the view that the B-1 is important for this purpose.[9] Other government spokesmen, however, have minimized these contributions or have omitted bombers entirely from calculations of the strategic balance. They may have done so because bomber payloads and missile throw-weights are not commensurable, because the Interim Agreement on strategic offensive arms does not limit bombers,[10] or because bombers are opposed by widespread Soviet air defenses.

On still another plane, the Vladivostok agreement heightens the negative political image of bombers by putting them in the same category as strategic missiles that do not carry MIRVs, even though each B-52G/H and each B-1 can carry more warheads than any U.S. or Soviet ballistic missile. Ironically, much of the critical comment on the force balance tentatively established by the Vladivostok agreement emphasizes the throw-weight advantage of the MIRV-carrying missiles the Soviet Union would probably retain under any future accord based on the agreement but ignores the advantages that the bomber force gives to the United States in the category of forces without MIRVs.

Despite these ambiguities in the perceptions of the political utility of the bomber force, the United States has few alternatives other than bombers with which to balance Soviet advantages in ballistic missile numbers and throw-weight. Asymmetrical limits on the number and size of ICBM silos in the 1972 Interim Agreement are almost certain to be incorporated in any new agreement stemming from the Vladivostok guidelines and in effect would prohibit the United States from catching up in the amount of throw-weight carried by ballistic missiles, both with and without MIRVs. Thus, unless the United States either declares essential equivalence inconsequential or can be satisfied by possessing equal numbers of missiles with and without MIRVs, the bomber force will have to be the counterweight to larger Soviet missiles.

9. For the "essential equivalence" argument, see statement of John L. McLucas, secretary of the Air Force, "Department of the Air Force Presentation to the Committee on Appropriations, United States Senate, Budget Estimates for Fiscal Year 1975" (March 7, 1974; processed), pp. 5–6.

10. Interim Agreement between the United States of America and the Union of Soviet Socialist Republics on Certain Measures with Respect to the Limitation of Strategic Offensive Arms, signed at Moscow, May 26, 1972.

Table 2-1. Possible U.S. Forces under the Vladivostok Guidelines

Force	Number[a]
MIRV-carrying missiles	
Poseidon (or Trident I in Poseidon submarines)	496
Minuteman III	550
Trident I or II in Trident submarines	240
Subtotal (Vladivostok limit: 1,320)	1,286
Bombers and missiles without MIRVs	
B-52G/H	270
B-52D	80
Minuteman II	450
Polaris	160
Titan	54
FB-111[b]	75
Subtotal	1,089
Total (Vladivostok limit: 2,400)	2,375

a. As of September 1975, 400 Poseidon missiles were deployed. All of the Minuteman IIIs were deployed as of July 1975.

b. It is not clear whether the FB-111s will be counted in the agreement resulting from the Vladivostok guidelines.

The Vladivostok guidelines would set a ceiling on U.S. forces in excess of present plans. If the United States decides to build up to the prescribed overall level of 2,400 delivery vehicles and 1,320 MIRV-carrying missiles, it can do so by retaining existing delivery vehicles and adding the 240 Trident launchers now planned. Additional bombers are not needed for this purpose. Table 2-1 illustrates these points.

The Bomber's Role in Nuclear Warfighting

We previously pointed out that the United States does not buy nuclear forces for warfighting in excess of those needed for deterrence. It is nevertheless instructive to examine the force characteristics needed for warfighting in order to assess the extent to which they are possessed by strategic bombers. Most discussions of these characteristics center on the accuracy needed in U.S. ballistic missiles, but other properties may be even more important. Among them are:

ENDURING SURVIVABILITY. Nuclear warfighting might consist of both fighting and negotiating. The latter would be greatly facilitated if U.S. national leaders could negotiate secure in the knowledge that their unexpended nuclear forces could be withheld for possible later use without seriously risking the loss of the forces or of command and control over them.

RETARGETABILITY. How nuclear war might break out is highly uncertain. Consequently the United States might want to change its war plans once actual hostilities began; the ability to reassign nuclear weapons to new targets quickly and accurately would be valuable.

SMALL-ATTACK UTILITY. Nuclear war might involve small attacks to obtain certain military and psychological effects. Weapons well-suited for such use would be ones that have high unit effectiveness, thus permitting the United States to use only a few weapons instead of many and still remain confident in the success of the mission.

SPEED OF RESPONSE. Weapons that do not have to be committed until just before they are needed on targets would in general be preferred to weapons that must be committed long before they are needed.

ABILITY TO RELOAD. It would be desirable to be able to reload bombers or missile launchers used in limited attacks so that all U.S. forces would be available for warfighting operations if hostilities expanded.

The military criteria implied by these warfighting roles for strategic offensive forces seem to be best fulfilled by missiles, not by bombers. Missiles are faster than bombers, equally accurate, easier to retarget, and less vulnerable to defenses, and their unit effectiveness in small attacks is higher and better protected by existing strategic arms control agreements. With appropriate advance planning—for example, advance procurement and positioning of missiles—ICBM and SLBM launchers could be reloaded. SLBMs, especially, are better adapted for enduring survivability.[11] Thus it seems fair to conclude that if the United States were to change its policy and decide to procure forces over and above those now bought for deterrence or essential equivalence to meet warfighting criteria, missiles would be a better choice for this purpose than bombers.

Secondary Considerations in Assessing the Need for Bombers

Some advocates of strategic bombers cite the effects the bomber force has on U.S. conventional warfare capabilities, on Soviet attack planning and air defense decisions, and on U.S. strategic flexibility. We believe

11. Secretary of Defense Schlesinger said that "our sea-launched ballistic missile (SLBM) force provides us, for the foreseeable future, with a high confidence capability to withhold weapons in reserve." ("Report on the FY 1976 and Transition Budgets," p. I-14.)

these arguments are secondary to both the deterrence and essential equivalence rationales that are discussed above but include them here in an effort to present all points of view.

The Bomber Force and Conventional Warfare

The use of B-52s in Vietnam is usually cited as evidence of the utility of strategic bombers in conventional warfare. B-52 bomber operations in Vietnam can be divided into two categories: those in South Vietnam, a theater in which there was no air defense of any consequence, and those in North Vietnam, where air defenses were strong by conventional warfare standards and where the B-52s rarely ventured until the Christmas bombing of 1972.

In South Vietnam the B-52s unquestionably added to U.S. conventional capabilities in that they were able to deliver large conventional bomb loads into relatively small areas in a short period of time. But the construction of a new modern bomber such as the B-1 would be difficult to justify on the basis of this argument. Were such capabilities required again, either the B-52s or some less sophisticated bomber aircraft would be more than sufficient to carry out the task; old aircraft such as the B-52Ds could be retained as part of the Tactical Air Command for such operations.

In North Vietnam, on the other hand, the B-52s encountered relatively severe attrition over Hanoi, about 3 percent by some estimates.[12] Air operations could not be sustained for long if air defenses continued to extract attrition at these rates. For example, at a 3 percent attrition rate, 50 percent of a given bomber force would be destroyed after only twenty-three missions. At 5 percent, it would take only fourteen missions. *Extended* campaigns by strategic bombers against modern air defenses may thus be infeasible, and only extended campaigns can hope to achieve important military results when conventional explosives are used. Short air operations intended to achieve psychological or political results might be successful, or bombers using the new precision-guided munitions, such as "smart bombs," could destroy selected high-value targets. Again, however, we believe it would be difficult to rationalize a program as expensive as the B-1 on this basis. Indeed this rationale has not been emphasized by supporters of the B-1.

12. Alton H. Quanbeck and Barry M. Blechman, *Strategic Forces: Issues for the Mid-Seventies* (Brookings Institution, 1973), p. 90.

The Bomber Force and Soviet Attack Planning

Another argument is that the strategic bomber force creates an attack-timing problem for the Soviet Union. An alert bomber force can be attacked successfully only by weapons whose approach cannot be detected in time to permit the aircraft to take off and escape. As a practical matter this means that the USSR would have to rely on missiles launched from submarines patrolling near the U.S. coast. For the foreseeable future an attack on the U.S. ICBM force, however, would have to be made with Soviet ICBMs because only they are likely to have the yield and accuracy needed. Since the flight time of ICBMs is about thirty minutes and that of SLBMs is only seven to fifteen minutes, an attack-planning problem would arise.

The Soviet Union could schedule the launches of its ICBMs and SLBMs so that the missiles would arrive at their targets at the same time (in which case Soviet ICBMs would be launched first), or it could schedule the missiles to be launched at the same time (in which case Soviet SLBMs would arrive at U.S. bomber bases fifteen to twenty minutes before the ICBMs would arrive at U.S. ICBM fields). The Soviet Union would almost certainly not adopt the first approach, since the resulting thirty minutes of warning would virtually guarantee the survival of the U.S. strategic bomber force, and the United States might still launch its ICBMs on warning of a massive attack by the USSR. Thus the second possibility is the one usually discussed. It is argued that if the United States were prepared to launch its ICBMs once Soviet SLBM warheads began exploding over U.S. bomber bases (but before Soviet ICBMs arrived), a Soviet disarming strike would not be possible even if the bombers were vulnerable. The bomber force would therefore have enhanced the survivability of an otherwise vulnerable ICBM force and precluded a Soviet calculation that a disarming strike against U.S. strategic forces would be possible. This argument has a number of weaknesses.

First, a disarming strike is impossible as long as any one of the three components of the U.S. strategic forces—ICBMs, SLBMs, or bombers—is survivable. All three are now, and most authorities expect at least the SLBMs to remain survivable far into the future. Moreover, should sufficient warning be available, part of the bomber force could be put on airborne alert, which would also preclude a disarming strike.

Second, the argument imposes no requirements on the bomber force other than that a portion of it be on alert and that this portion be large enough not to be ignored in Soviet attack planning. Even relatively primitive bombers would serve this purpose.

Third, if the criteria implied by this argument were incorporated into U.S. force planning, quite different decisions on U.S. ICBM and bomber forces would result. For example, the United States would not need to devote much effort to increasing the hardness of its ICBM silos; instead it would concentrate on the development of both rapid-reaction capabilities for the ICBMs and better warning and attack assessment systems to ensure the launching of the ICBM force. In the case of the bomber force, logic would require giving the force only the sacrificial role of a trip wire to enable the United States to launch its ICBMs. Thus the bomber force would need to be only good enough and big enough to be a threat if it is not attacked. The United States could almost certainly reduce the costs of the current bomber force were it to depend solely on these synergistic effects of bombers and ICBMs.

Fourth, should the Soviet Union decide to carry out a surprise attack, it would probably choose to do so when it would be difficult for American leaders to reach a decision to launch U.S. ICBMs in the very short time available—during a domestic crisis, for example.

Fifth, even if the United States could launch its ICBMs in these circumstances, and did so, it would then be employing a policy of fast response, which would be inconsistent with strategies intended to limit nuclear violence if deterrence should fail and to bring nuclear hostilities to a speedy conclusion before catastrophic damage resulted.

On balance it appears that, at most, the complications in Soviet attack planning created by the bomber force only add to the vast uncertainties already inherent in any first-strike calculations the USSR might make.

The Bomber Force and Soviet Spending on Air Defense

The Soviet Union has maintained a large air defense system for many years. The system currently consists of about 12,000 surface-to-air missiles and about 2,600 manned interceptors, all supported by a vast network of about 4,000 surveillance radars.[13] Nevertheless, senior U.S. Air Force officers and defense officials are confident that U.S. strategic bombers could penetrate to targets in the USSR (see chapter 5). These views have

13. Ibid., p. II-19.

been reinforced by experience in Vietnam and the Middle East. In those conflicts, air operations against Soviet-built air defenses suggest that the latter would be relatively ineffective in a nuclear war. Even high attrition rates for attacking bombers—rates not even approached in Vietnam or the Middle East—would still permit bombers armed with nuclear weapons to inflict catastrophic damage on defended targets.

In addition, the Soviet air defense system is vulnerable to suppression attacks by U.S. ballistic missiles. It is therefore unlikely that Soviet air defenses, in a *massive* U.S.-Soviet nuclear war, would frustrate U.S. air operations. On the other hand, Soviet air defenses might work well against a small bomber attack carried out as part of a limited nuclear war. In contrast, Soviet defenses would be totally ineffective against a small ballistic missile attack.

Why the USSR maintains a large and expensive air defense system is uncertain. It is probable that in the past at least, the Soviet Union primarily has responded—however ineffectively—to the threat posed by the bombers of the U.S. Strategic Air Command. It could be, however, that if the U.S. strategic bomber force were reduced or permitted to obsolesce, the air forces of the North Atlantic Treaty Organization and the People's Republic of China might continue to justify the maintenance of the Soviet air defense system. Alternatively, Soviet leaders might prefer that the United States spend money modernizing its bomber forces rather than its ballistic missile forces. They may believe that by maintaining their air defenses they are inducing the United States to allocate money to a type of nuclear delivery system—bombers—that in Soviet eyes is less threatening than missiles. It is also possible that bureaucratic inertia dominates Soviet air defense programs. But if the USSR is driven mainly by concern about the U.S. strategic bomber force, the present force is sufficient to encourage major modernization of Soviet air defenses.

In sum, U.S. defense planners do not know the precise relationship between Soviet air defense policies and decisions the United States might make about the bomber force, and in the authors' view the correlation between the two is insufficient to justify maintaining the bomber force.

The Bomber Force and Strategic Flexibility

It is correctly argued that in crises the bomber force alert rate can be increased or that some of the bombers can be put on airborne alert as gestures of U.S. resolve and commitment. It is further argued that strategic bombers are particularly well-suited for limited nuclear strikes because they are highly reliable, can accurately deliver low-yield weapons that would minimize collateral damage, can be kept under close control throughout an attack, and can report results back immediately. According to a senior spokesman for the Air Force, Lieutenant General James R. Allen, bombers provide "a mode of attack which will allow the enemy to discern unmistakably that he is indeed facing only a limited response by the United States."[14]

But in considering small attacks against the Soviet Union involving only a few bombers, one must take into account the extensive air defenses deployed there. Although Soviet air defenses would not offer much opposition to massive attacks, they would be much more formidable during light attacks involving only a few bombers. Therefore to be sure that at least one bomber would penetrate to the target in a limited strike, it might be necessary to use a relatively large number of attacking aircraft. Such an operation not only could confuse the Soviet Union about U.S. intentions but might be relatively costly in the number of aircraft the United States might lose.

On the other hand, no effective defense against ICBMs or SLBMs has yet been deployed in the Soviet Union, nor is one likely to be, because there are technical and economic barriers to the construction of such defenses and because the ABM treaty and the 1974 Protocol limit their construction.[15] SLBMs and ICBMs can respond quicker than bombers to the command to attack. Because of their short time of flight—fifteen and thirty minutes, respectively—the missiles need not be committed until just before target destruction is desired. Strategic bombers, of course, would have to be committed several hours earlier. With respect to accuracy, it has been reported that the circular error probable (CEP) of some current U.S. ballistic missiles is about 1,500 feet, and it is possible that improvements to present Minuteman guidance systems might result in CEPs of

14. Statement in *Fiscal Year 1975 Authorization for Military Procurement, Research and Development, and Active Duty, Selected Reserve and Civilian Personnel Strengths,* Hearings before the Senate Armed Services Committee, 93 Cong. 2 sess. (1974), pt. 7, p. 3874.

15. Treaty between the United States of America and the Union of Soviet Socialist Republics on the Limitation of Anti-Ballistic Missile Systems, signed at Moscow, May 26, 1972; and Protocol to the Treaty . . . on the Limitation of Anti-Ballistic Missile Systems, signed at Moscow, July 3, 1974.

700 feet.[16] Even better CEPs might be obtained by using maneuvering terminally guided reentry vehicles. Thus even current ballistic missiles may be accurate enough to successfully attack all but very hard targets with relatively low-yield weapons. With the advent of even better accuracies, perhaps measured in tens of feet for terminally guided reentry vehicles, no fixed target will be immune to ballistic missile attack. Consequently the ability to attack a full range of targets would not be unique to the bomber. It appears that current or future bombers will have little advantage over ballistic missiles with regard to accuracy, especially if bomber attacks involve air-to-surface missiles such as short-range attack missiles (SRAMs).

Another argument is that bombers can be launched on warning under positive control and can be recalled if desired. This is indeed an attribute that is not possessed by other strategic forces. It should be noted, however, that this reasoning tries to turn a liability—the *necessity* that bombers maintained on ground alert be launched on warning of attack if they are to survive—into a virtue. Unlike ICBMs and SLBMs, bombers cannot ride out an attack on their bases. Were ground alert bombers not recallable, they would not be acceptable components of U.S. strategic forces.

Finally, the point is often made that bombers are reliable and combat tested and as a consequence are more dependable than missiles. Bombers, however, have not engaged in nuclear combat against nuclear-armed defenses, and air-to-surface missiles, such as SRAMs, have not been tested any more extensively than Minuteman, Polaris, or Poseidon. Uncertainties about bomber performance in a nuclear war therefore remain unresolved—just as in the case of strategic missiles. Coupled with Soviet air defenses, these factors suggest that it is at best unclear whether bombers are in fact more reliable than ballistic missiles for limited attacks.[17]

16. Clarence A. Robinson, Jr., "U.S. Plans 'Cold Launch' ICBMs," *Aviation Week and Space Technology,* vol. 100 (February 4, 1974), p. 14. Quanbeck and Blechman have explained CEP as being "the commonest measure of the accuracy with which a ballistic missile can deliver its reentry vehicles. It is defined as the radius of a circle centered on the target within which 50 percent of the reentry vehicles would impact if the test were repeated many times. Thus, if a ballistic missile system is said to have a CEP of 1 nautical mile, its reentry vehicles would have a 50 percent probability of landing within a circle of 1 nautical mile radius, centered on the target." (*Strategic Forces,* p. 72.)

17. Tests of operational Minuteman missiles out of Vandenberg Air Force Base, California, have been highly successful, but limited unrepresentative tests out of operational launchers have been much less so. Because launches of SLBMs could reveal submarine location, SLBMs are less likely to be used for limited attacks. It

How Big a Task Should the Bomber Force Be Designed to Do?

If, as has been argued, the purpose of the bomber force is primarily to ensure against the failure of the ICBMs and SLBMs, how much insurance should the United States buy for this purpose? The bomber force the United States needs depends on several factors: the task assigned to it, the number of aircraft expected to survive attack by Soviet offensive weapons, and the extent to which Soviet air defenses might degrade the bomber force as it carries out its mission.

In our opinion, the bomber force should be designed and sized to attack fixed industrial and urban targets. This would be consistent not only with the capabilities of the bomber force but also with the basic notion that bombers serve as a hedge against the failure of the other retaliatory forces. Thus a reasonably clear though arbitrary upper limit on the size of the task for the bomber force can be determined. About 400 1-megaton weapons, or weapons of equivalent yield, could destroy about three-fourths of the industrial capacity of the Soviet Union and about one-third of its population. Increments of force above this level would yield relatively small returns in additional damage. This amount of destruction can be inflicted by the delivery of about 1,200 reliable 200-kiloton warheads—the yield that might be carried by modern air-to-surface missiles.[18] Allowances must be made, however, for unreliable airplanes and missiles, penetration aids, and attrition by enemy offensive and defensive forces.

Maintaining essential equivalence might also be considered in designing the strategic bomber force. Table 2-1 shows that there are about 750 older delivery systems (B-52Ds, Minuteman IIs, Polaris, and Titans, all without MIRVs) that might have to be replaced in the next ten or fifteen years. Ideally, at some future time agreed mutual reductions would eliminate many of these old missiles from the forces of both sides. Barring such reductions, however, and assuming that limits on MIRV-carrying missiles

---

may very well be that no U.S. strategic delivery system has been sufficiently tested to give strategists high confidence in the results of a limited attack by one or two such weapons. This is one of the reasons why tactical aircraft might be more attractive for this purpose.

18. Equivalent yield is a measure of the ability of a nuclear weapon to destroy a soft, distributed target, such as a city. It is calculated by raising the yield of a weapon to the ⅔ power. The equivalent yield of a 200-kiloton weapon is therefore about 0.34 megaton; 1,200 such weapons would have an equivalent yield of about 400 megatons.

are not increased in any follow-on agreement, the United States could face the need to deploy many new strategic bombers to keep forces near the limit of 2,400 set at Vladivostok.[19] At least three approaches might be taken to replacing the older delivery systems.

First, the natural desire to achieve high unit performance in numerically limited forces might be permitted to dominate the U.S. approach to modernizing the missiles and bombers lacking MIRVs. This could lead to highly capable but extremely costly forces. The B-1 and the standoff missile carriers discussed later in this study are examples of systems with high unit cost and high unit effectiveness.

Second, the United States could develop a less expensive bomber, which if deployed in sufficient numbers would meet U.S. strategic objectives and maintain U.S. forces near the Vladivostok limit of 2,400. But no bomber now being seriously considered in this study or elsewhere appears to be well-suited to this approach.

The third approach would be the same as the first except that less emphasis would be put on deploying delivery vehicles to meet the agreed numerical ceiling and more emphasis would be given to the *capabilities* of deployed vehicles. The capability needed for deterrence would be determined and obtained in the most economically efficient way. In chapter 6, where we compare forces of equal effectiveness, the task is to deliver the equivalent of 400 1-megaton weapons. We could have specified a larger task without affecting the broad trade-offs among alternative bomber forces.

Is Modernizing the Strategic Bomber Force Urgent?

The arguments advanced so far that favor the retention of an adequate strategic bomber force do not present compelling reasons to build a new force now. In presenting his annual report to Congress in 1975, Defense Secretary Schlesinger suggested that the Soviet Union would not acquire a "significant hard target kill capability" before the early 1980s and that this would occur even later if the new Soviet missiles equipped with

19. The United States could deploy additional missiles without MIRVs, but this would entail developing the missiles or resuming the production of old ones. The temptation to deploy bombers of more recent design and with larger payloads of air-to-surface missiles (bomber MIRVs, if you will) would, in our view, prove irresistible in this situation.

MIRVs initially lack sufficient accuracy.[20] In any event, U.S. defense planners have anticipated the achievement of this capability by initiating the Trident program, and the survivability prospects for U.S. SSBNs, as we have argued, are excellent into the foreseeable future. Deployment of the ten planned Trident submarines can bring U.S. forces essentially into line with the limits set at Vladivostok and shown in table 2-1. Thus the United States can maintain approximate equality under the Vladivostok agreement without a new bomber force.

A final consideration is the condition of the present bomber force. The B-52G/Hs are thoroughly modern aircraft even though their lineage can be traced back to the mid-1950s. They are equipped with modern armament—both SRAMs and bombs. The weapon loads on the B-52G/Hs could be more than doubled by loading wing pylons with twelve more SRAMs, air-launched cruise missiles, or armed decoys. (The latter two weapons, of course, do not exist now.) Furthermore, the B-52G/Hs are undergoing modernization of their electronic countermeasures systems at a cost of about $350 million.[21]

The B-52G/Hs have been equipped with quick-start accessories to improve prelaunch survivability and with electro-optical viewing systems (TV) to improve low-altitude performance by providing a view outside and forward of the aircraft when the cockpit is hooded to protect the crew from bright flashes created by nuclear explosions. The B-52G/Hs are expected to remain structurally sound into the 1990s. Current Defense Department plans call for retaining the B-52G/Hs even after the B-1s are deployed. Thus the B-52G/Hs appear capable of performing all the desired roles of a manned strategic bomber force for many years, subject to the uncertainty about their vulnerability to surprise attacks while they are on ground alert and to air defenses, matters treated at length in chapters 4 and 5.

Summary

The United States now has and expects to retain large, capable ballistic missile forces. These are nearly certain to have substantial retaliatory capabilities far into the future. Moreover, the United States has anticipated

20. See "Report on the FY 1976 and Transition Budgets," p. II-14.
21. "USAF Stresses B-1 Penetration Ability," *Aviation Week and Space Technology,* vol. 102 (January 27, 1975), p. 97.

the foreseeable problems that the strategic ballistic missiles might encounter. Barring technological breakthroughs, it is likely that the ballistic missile forces, *in aggregate,* will retain into the 1990s roughly the retaliatory capabilities they now possess, although the SLBMs will probably carry more of this retaliatory burden than they do now. Thus, for the deterrence mission, bombers are justified primarily as insurance against unexpected technological breakthroughs that might weaken the retaliatory capability of missiles.

Soviet ballistic missile forces are larger than those of the United States, however. The existing U.S. bomber force can therefore be thought of as a political counterweight to these Soviet missile capabilities. But essential equivalence is speculative and subjective in definition; no empirical basis for judging its importance has been advanced, and criteria by which to measure it are nebulous and ill-defined. The importance of essential equivalence rests on the premise that differential strategic nuclear capabilities that have little or no military value may nevertheless have important political value. Despite the ill-defined nature of essential equivalence, we believe that the United States should keep forces that in practice are widely believed to be essentially equivalent. Unfortunately, the essential equivalence concept provides no clear basis for objectively determining the proper size of the bomber force.

On balance, we believe that there is a case for retaining a bomber force, and the United States is committed to doing so. The practical question is how this might best be done.

CHAPTER THREE

THE PRESENT COURSE

B-29 bombers delivered the two atomic bombs of approximately 20-kiloton yield that fell on the Japanese cities of Hiroshima and Nagasaki near the end of World War II. From that time until the deployment of a substantial number of long-range ballistic missiles in the early 1960s, bombers were the primary delivery means for U.S. strategic nuclear forces. The Soviet Union also relied mainly on bombers to carry its nuclear weapons until ballistic missiles became available. The Soviet bomber force, however, has been smaller in size, has possessed less modern aircraft, and has remained at a lower state of readiness than the bomber force of the United States.

Table 3-1 shows the number of active aircraft in the U.S. bomber and tanker force from 1960 to the present. In fiscal year 1960 the bomber force consisted of over 1,900 aircraft of the B-52 and B-47 types and over 1,200 tankers—a mix of KC-135s, which are military tanker versions of the Boeing 707, and propeller-driven KC-97s. These were deployed at approximately sixty bases in the United States, Europe, and the Pacific.[1] During the early 1960s the readiness and manning of the bomber force were such that one-eighth of the force could have been maintained on airborne alert for one year; half the bomber force was kept on fifteen-minute ground alert.[2]

In fiscal 1975, on the other hand, the bomber/tanker force consisted of five squadrons of older model B-52D/Fs, eighteen squadrons of B-52G/Hs, four squadrons of FB-111s, and thirty-eight KC-135 squadrons, each squadron equipped with about fifteen aircraft. Each bomber

1. "Statement of Secretary of Defense Robert S. McNamara before the House Armed Services Committee on the Fiscal Year 1965–69 Defense Program and 1965 Defense Budget" (January 27, 1964; processed), p. 31.

2. Ibid., pp. 33, 36.

Table 3-1. U.S. Bomber and Tanker Force, Selected Fiscal Years

| | *Fiscal year* | | | | |
Aircraft	*1960*	*1964*	*1968*	*1972*	*1975*
Bombers	1,941	1,364	714	528	504
Tankers	1,230	998	667	661	661

Sources: "USAF Almanac," *Air Force*, vol. 56 (May 1973), p. 151; and "An Air Force Almanac," *Air Force*, vol. 57 (May 1974), p. 139.

squadron generally occupies one Strategic Air Command (SAC) base and is frequently colocated with a tanker squadron. Thus there are now about twenty-three primary bases in the United States and an additional seventy military and civil air bases to which the bombers can be dispersed in time of crisis.[3] For the past several years about 40 percent of the bomber and tanker force has been kept on ground alert status.[4] The airborne alert capability of the present bomber force is probably somewhat less than that of the force in the early 1960s as evidenced by the lower level of manning for ground alert. In February 1975 the secretary of defense announced a plan to further reduce the day-to-day alert rate to 30 percent on the grounds that a Soviet surprise attack is quite unlikely and that U.S. missile capability has been increased. Consequently the ratio of air crews to aircraft can be reduced from about 1:6 to 1:3.[5]

Systems and Costs

The performance of the bomber force depends on the characteristics of the bombers and their armament as well as on the number of bombers in the force, but choices among competing alternatives should be based on consideration of their costs as well. Here, therefore, we discuss the characteristics and costs of bombers and their weapons, covering systems cur-

3. *Fiscal Year 1975 Authorization for Military Procurement, Research and Development, and Active Duty, Selected Reserve and Civilian Personnel Strengths,* Hearings before the Senate Armed Services Committee, 93 Cong. 2 sess. (1974), pt. 7, p. 3942. For a map showing the locations of the SAC bases, see *Air Force,* vol. 57 (May 1974), p. 151.

4. *Military Implications of the Treaty on the Limitation of Strategic Offensive Arms,* Hearings before the Senate Armed Services Committee, 92 Cong. 2 sess. (1972), p. 474.

5. "Report of Secretary of Defense James R. Schlesinger to the Congress on the FY 1976 and Transition Budgets, FY 1977 Authorization Request and FY 1976–1980 Defense Programs" (February 5, 1975; processed), pp. II-35–II-36.

rently deployed, systems now in development, and certain systems that could be developed within roughly the next five years for deployment in the 1980s.[6]

The B-52 Boeing Stratofortress

The first prototype B-52 flew in April 1952, beginning a long series of models that have constituted the major part of the U.S. airborne deterrent force up until the present. A total of 744 production models were delivered to the Air Force between 1954 and 1962; about 330 are expected to remain operational. Approximately seventy-five aircraft in this fleet are B-52D models that were delivered in the 1956–58 period. The D-model bombers are undergoing modifications to their wings to correct structural deficiencies at a cost of $240 million.[7] The remaining portion of the B-52 fleet consists of G and H models. The G models, first deployed in 1959, were improved in both range (up to 10,000 miles unrefueled) and defensive capability with the addition of a remotely controlled tail turret gun. Turbofan engines were incorporated in the H model enabling the aircraft to set a new distance record of over 12,500 miles for unrefueled flight.[8]

The B-52G/H aircraft are being modified to carry up to twenty short-range attack missiles (SRAMs), twelve under the wings and eight in a rotary dispenser in the aft bomb bay. In addition each aircraft can carry four Mark-28 gravity nuclear bombs in the forward bomb bay for a maximum payload of twenty-four weapons. Each B-52 carries an air crew of six. Approximately $210 million is still required to strengthen the wing structure on the remaining B-52D aircraft and to complete the modification of B-52G/H aircraft to carry SRAM missiles, to provide a quick-start capability for their engines, and to improve the electronic countermeasures equipment.

In particular, SAC has undertaken an extensive program to modify and

6. We derived the performance information from *Jane's All the World's Aircraft* and various technical journals; cost estimates are from Department of Defense budget publications and Air Force testimony before congressional committees. In some instances, because cost data were not available from these sources, we made our own estimates.

7. *Department of Defense Appropriations: Fiscal Year 1975*, Hearings before the Senate Committee on Appropriations, 93 Cong. 2 sess. (1974), pt. 4, p. 570.

8. Range figures quoted here and elsewhere in this chapter may not be strictly comparable. Useful bomber range is a complex function of payload, flight profile, and other factors. The figures cited serve as a rough indicator of potential aircraft range performance.

augment the electronic countermeasure capability of the B-52 in order to counter Soviet air defense radars. SAC views this as a principal means of extending the useful life of the B-52 fleet.[9]

The Air Force considered a Boeing proposal to further modify G and H models with new engines, a supercritical wing, an extended bomb bay, improved avionics, low-level ride control, and provisions for a four-man crew.[10] These steps would have cost about $40 million in current dollars per aircraft, however, and the Air Force decided not to modify the B-52s.

Most of the costs of the B-52 force are now associated with its operations and maintenance. We estimate that the direct operating cost for a squadron of B-52s is about $40 million annually. This includes the pay of military and civilian personnel in the operational units and bases,[11] the cost of fuel and other consumables, and the repair and maintenance of aircraft and other equipment. Direct operating costs can be considered to be variable to the extent that they vary directly with the number of units. The elimination or addition of one unit should result in a proportional change in direct operating costs within a year or so.

Indirect operating costs include shared costs for the training of aircrews and personnel, higher headquarters such as the Pentagon, operational central depots for supply and maintenance, intelligence collection, and medical care for military personnel and their dependents. Some of these indirect costs are fixed and would not vary with changes in the size and composition of the bomber force. Others, such as costs for training crews and overhaul depots, will change with force size. Our calculations show that the indirect operating costs for the B-52 force are nearly equal to the direct operating costs.

The FB-111A

The FB-111A is a strategic bomber version of the variable sweep F-111 fighter-bomber produced by General Dynamics. It is limited in range (only 4,100 miles) and in payload (up to four SRAMs on external pylons

9. "USAF Stresses B-1 Penetration Ability," *Aviation Week and Space Technology,* vol. 102 (January 27, 1975), p. 97.

10. "B-1 Development Program," Statement of Honorable John L. McLucas, Secretary of the Air Force, Presentation to the Senate Armed Services Committee, Research and Development Subcommittee (April 17, 1975; processed).

11. There are approximately 1,100 officers and enlisted men in a B-52 squadron. See *Fiscal Year 1975 Authorization for Military Procurement,* Hearings, pt. 4, p. 1579.

and two in the bomb bay) and carries a crew of two. The aircraft has a supersonic speed capability of Mach 2.5 at high altitude. Its costs, like those of the B-52 force, are now mainly direct and indirect operating costs. There are approximately 350 fewer personnel in an FB-111A squadron than in a B-52 squadron, and its operating costs should run approximately 35 percent less annually.

The B-1

The design of the B-1 was based on the initial concept of the advanced manned strategic aircraft (AMSA). The original studies of the AMSA date back to 1962; by 1965 the Air Force had formalized the design concept and the range of performance specifications. Now, some ten years later, the first prototype of the new manned bomber is in its flight-test program.

The specifications, particularly the requirement for supersonic speed at both high and low altitude, that were advanced for the AMSA led to the incorporation in the B-1 of variable-geometry wing technology like that of the F-111, which was being developed in the early 1960s. The wings swing from a full forward position of 15-degree sweep to a fully swept position of 65 degrees. A low-altitude-ride-control system has been incorporated into the aircraft to dampen the adverse effects of turbulence on the structure and the crew during low-altitude flight. The nominal unrefueled range of the B-1 is reported to be about 6,100 miles.[12]

The primary armament for the B-1 is expected to be the SRAM. A maximum of twenty-four SRAMs can be carried in the aircraft's three identical rotary launchers. Utilizing its terrain-following radar, the B-1 can penetrate at altitudes as low as 100 feet and at speeds up to about 400 knots.[13] It is anticipated that the radar cross section of the B-1 will be one-tenth that of the B-52, although its infrared signature will be somewhat larger due to the greater thrust of its engines and its higher speed.[14] Plans for engine infrared suppression devices have been eliminated for technical and cost reasons, thus increasing the vulnerability of the aircraft

12. S. H. H. Young, "Gallery of USAF Weapons," *Air Force,* vol. 57 (May 1974), p. 112.

13. J. Philip Geddes, "Progress on the B-1 Bomber," *International Defense Review,* vol. 4 (August 1971), p. 344.

14. Ibid. A heat source emits infrared radiation that lies outside the visible spectrum. The emissive power varies with the temperature of the heat source. Infrared sensors can be used to detect and home in on this radiation.

to infrared-seeking missiles, but this may not be of much consequence since the B-1 would penetrate at low altitude. Radar cross section is the more significant measure of susceptibility to detection in the low-altitude flight regime.

A number of the early specifications for the bomber have been relaxed to limit increases in both cost and weight. The requirement for supersonic speed at low altitude has been reduced to the high subsonic range. The B-1 can still reach Mach 2.2 at high altitude, but this supersonic capability would be useful to the strategic mission in only a limited set of situations since the B-1's primary penetration tactic is flight at low altitude to avoid detection by enemy ground-based radars. The takeoff weight of the aircraft has increased from a planned 360,000 pounds to 395,000 pounds.[15] This increase in weight has had two adverse effects: the takeoff distance has increased from 6,500 to 7,500 feet and the aircraft's range has been diminished by 7 to 8 percent.[16] In a recent change, the crew escape capsule was eliminated from the production version to avoid added cost after it was learned that the capsule became unstable when separated at more than 300 knots. The aircraft will be equipped with ejection seats instead.

The overall effect of these trade-offs between cost and performance was assessed in 1973 by a committee under the chairmanship of Raymond L. Bisplinghoff that was convened by the secretary of the Air Force to investigate the B-1 program. The Bisplinghoff Committee reported that in ten out of eleven important performance parameters the B-1 would fail to meet its original development estimate. The most probable reduction in the design performance averaged over 11 percent for eleven categories.[17] But despite these reductions in performance the B-1 can be expected to meet the primary mission requirements for which it was designed.

Much of the controversy over the B-1 stems from the high cost of the program. Table 3-2 illustrates the growth in the cost estimates for the B-1 presented by the Air Force in testimony before the Senate Appropriations Committee.[18] These estimates in 1970 dollars show a real cost growth of about 16 percent between 1969 and 1974.

The most recent official estimate of the B-1 program costs now has exceeded $20 billion in current dollars.[19] On that basis, the acquisition of

15. *Fiscal Year 1975 Authorization for Military Procurement,* Hearings, pt. 7, pp. 3979–80.

16. Ibid., pp. 3942, 3978.

17. *Department of Defense Appropriations, 1975,* Hearings, pt. 4, p. 575.

18. Ibid.

19. *Defense Space Business Daily,* February 7, 1975.

Table 3-2. B-1 Cost Estimates for Selected Years
Millions of 1970 dollars

Item	1969	1970	1974
Development	1,947	2,431	3,030
Procurement	7,572	7,423	8,051
Total	9,519	9,854	11,081

Source: *Department of Defense Appropriations: Fiscal Year 1975*, Hearings before the Senate Committee on Appropriations, 93 Cong. 2 sess. (1974), pt. 4, p. 575.

244 aircraft would result in an average cost for each of $84 million, but *Aviation Week and Space Technology* has since reported that defense officials have told Congress that the bombers will cost more than $100 million each.[20]

Although operating costs for a B-1 squadron would be roughly the same as those for a B-52 squadron if the aircraft were maintained on the same alert status, the effect of the B-1 procurement program on the entire Air Force aircraft modernization program deserves special attention. During the past several years, the Air Force appropriation for aircraft procurement has remained relatively constant at nearly $3 billion annually. At that budget level the Air Force could procure on the average only 170 aircraft per year to modernize a total active force of over 8,000 aircraft.[21] If a corresponding modernization rate of 2 percent prevailed over a lengthy period of time, the Air Force would be faced with the undesirable choice of cutting force structure or flying obsolete aircraft well past their expected lifetimes. The high procurement costs of the B-1 are programmed to exceed $2 billion each year starting in fiscal year 1978 and can only exacerbate this modernization problem. Either the aircraft procurement appropriation must be drastically increased (at least doubled) by Congress or the Air Force must forgo modernization of its tactical air forces during the late seventies and early eighties.

Tankers

The KC-135 Stratotanker was developed from the prototype of the Boeing 707. Over 700 were built starting in 1956 for air-to-air refuelling of SAC bombers. Although they are under SAC's operational control,

20. Clarence A. Robinson, Jr., "USAF Manned Bomber Need Challenged," *Aviation Week and Space Technology*, March 24, 1975, p. 19.
21. For supporting data, see "An Air Force Almanac," *Air Force*, vol. 57 (May 1974), pp. 138–39.

they have been used extensively to refuel tactical fighters, particularly in Southeast Asia. A KC-135 tanker has the capacity to transfer up to 120,000 pounds of fuel; only one aircraft, however, can be refuelled at a time.

The Department of Defense has proposed the development of a new tanker/cargo aircraft. It is envisioned that this new tanker will involve the modification of a wide-body aircraft such as the Boeing 747, McDonnell Douglas DC-10, Lockheed L-1011, or C-5A. The advantages of this tanker would be its greater ability to transfer fuel, the probability that it could refuel two aircraft simultaneously, and its capacity to be used as a cargo aircraft for strategic airlifts. The Air Force estimates that it would cost about $225 million to develop the new tanker/cargo aircraft and that each modified wide-body transport aircraft would cost about $30 million.[22]

A tanker squadron requires only about half the personnel of a B-52 squadron; thus the operating costs per unit are substantially less for tankers than for bombers. A tanker is also flown less each month (about thirty-five hours as opposed to forty-five hours for B-52s) for purposes of maintaining crew combat readiness. There are now about three tankers, however, for each two bombers in the force structure, with the result that overall operating costs for tankers are about the same as for the present bomber force. Steps are being taken to transfer 128 tankers to the Air Force Reserve components.[23]

Air-to-Surface Missiles

The SRAM is a nuclear-armed supersonic missile that can be delivered from the parent bomber at ranges of up to 100 miles in a high-altitude semiballistic profile and of 35 miles at low altitude. Its very high speed (up to Mach 2.5) and small radar cross section render it practically invulnerable to an enemy defensive system once it has been launched. It has an inertial guidance system that is impossible to jam and that permits the launching of the missile at targets located straight ahead, sideways, or even to the rear of the launching aircraft. The yield of its warhead is reported to be comparable to a Minuteman III warhead of about 200 kilotons. The Air Force procured 1,500 SRAMs, but only 1,140 of these (known as "unit equipment") appear in tables of equipment assigned to operating units. The other 360 missiles provide a reserve for various pur-

22. *Department of Defense Appropriations, 1975,* Hearings, pt. 4, p. 53.
23. "Report on the FY 1976 and Transition Budgets," p. II-36.

poses; during a particular missile's life, it moves irregularly through various stages—sometimes assigned to an operational unit, sometimes undergoing extensive repair or modification. A relatively small number are also expended each year in operational tests.

The average unit procurement cost of these SRAM missiles (exclusive of the nuclear warhead) was $334,000.[24] But the production line was closed in 1975, and there would be start-up costs for producing SRAMs for the B-1 that are now estimated to be about $100 million. Adjusting for the effects of inflation since the time when production stopped, we estimate that future SRAM procurement costs would average $500,000 per missile in fiscal 1976 dollars.

A second air-to-surface missile, the air-launched cruise missile (ALCM), is being developed by the Air Force. The ALCM is essentially a modified subsonic cruise armed decoy (SCAD), a missile whose development was started by the Air Force in the late 1960s. Like the Navy's strategic cruise missile (SCM), the ALCM incorporates new technologies in propulsion and guidance. Lightweight turbofan engines, pioneered by the Williams Research Corporation and previously intended for the SCAD, enable a 2,000-pound ALCM to fly at ranges of up to 1,500 miles at high subsonic speeds.[25]

The navigation system of the ALCM uses terrain contour matching (TERCOM), a technique that has been extensively tested by both the Air Force and Navy.[26] The testimony of Navy spokesmen during hearings before the Senate Armed Services Committee indicated that cruise missiles equipped with TERCOM could have accuracies on the order of 0.1 nautical mile (600 feet) circular error probable.[27]

Because of the extended range of the cruise missiles, bombers equipped with them would not need to penetrate over enemy territory to launch their

24. *Fiscal Year 1975 Authorization for Military Procurement*, Hearings, pt. 7, p. 3726.

25. Ibid., p. 3636.

26. Captain W. M. Locke, USN, the strategic cruise missile project manager, described the system as follows:
"This system is based on the correlation of stored contour map data with the changes in the terrain being overflown as measured by a radar altimeter. Use of this data provides fixes at intervals along the route to the target. A series of such inertial legs, updated by the TERCOM system, has the potential for missile guidance accuracies of approximately [deleted] nautical-mile. The system has been extensively tested in captive flight, in real time, using maps prepared by the Defense Mapping Agency from data gathered by existing intelligence means." (Ibid.)

27. See ibid., pp. 3636, 3652.

missiles; thus it would be unnecessary for the bombers to descend to low altitude to avoid an adversary's defenses. The resulting change in flight profile would mean that on most operational missions from the United States to the Soviet Union, B-52G/H aircraft would not require air-to-air refueling. A simple geographic and demographic analysis shows that practically all of the Soviet Union's urban population is within 1,500 nautical miles of potential launch points outside the Soviet Union's borders. The deployment of such missiles on the B-52s or on a new missile-carrying aircraft is one alternative to the deployment of the B-1.

Two operational characteristics of the ALCM lead to the conclusion that they would penetrate even high-performance air defenses with relative impunity. First, the cruise missiles can fly at altitudes as low as 100 feet, and second, they can be designed to have a very low radar cross section.[28] Thus it is extremely unlikely that any land- or air-based radars would be able to detect them. The following exchange between Senator Thomas J. McIntyre of New Hampshire and Captain W. M. Locke, cruise missile project manager, illustrates the Navy's viewpoint:

SENATOR MCINTYRE. Considering all of the defenses deployed or postulated for the near future that the Soviets have or are thinking about, would it represent an expensive project for them to defend and defeat the cruise missiles we are talking about here this morning?

CAPTAIN LOCKE. Yes, sir. There is no existing defense against very low-flying cruise missiles. It would be extremely expensive to develop one; in the billions.[29]

The Air Force approached long-range cruise missiles through the SCAD program, which was conceived in 1967–68 soon after the feasibility of small, efficient turbofan engines and TERCOM guidance systems had been demonstrated. The purpose of SCAD was to accompany B-52s through air defenses, multiplying the number of penetrators by as much as ten or twelve and thereby saturating the air defenses. A substantial amount of work was done on the electronic countermeasures for SCAD and on the engine. System studies that defined a number of variants were also conducted. Some of these variants would have carried nuclear warheads; others would have been unarmed. They varied in size and hence in range capability. The Air Force favored smaller, relatively short-range unarmed variants.

In 1972 the Senate Armed Services Committee recommended approval of the SCAD program as a means of providing both a decoy and a cruise missile. The Air Force, however, proceeded to develop only decoy ca-

28. Ibid., pp. 3622, 3693.
29. Ibid., p. 3661.

pability and, according to the committee, "resisted pursuing SCAD with an armed warhead because of its possible use as a standoff missile. This application could jeopardize the B-1 program because it would not be necessary to have a bomber penetration if a standoff missile were available as a cheaper and more viable alternative."[30]

Finally, in 1973, the Department of Defense canceled the SCAD program. The reason given by the department was low cost-effectiveness.[31] This cancellation would have left the development of long-range cruise missiles to the Navy, whose submarine-launched missile program had been started in 1972 with money appropriated soon after the hearings on the strategic arms agreements. An Air Force cruise missile program was soon initiated as well, however; Congress appropriated $90 million for Air Force and Navy cruise missile programs in fiscal 1975, and the Defense Department's fiscal 1976 request includes money for both programs.

The Air Force is consistent, though, in emphasizing that the ALCM is a complement to the penetrating bomber, as this exchange between Senator McIntyre and Brigadier General Harold E. Confer of the Air Force staff indicates:

SENATOR MCINTYRE. In your opinion, could the cruise missile penetrate a defense comprised of extensive radar coverage including SUAWACS [Soviet Union Airborne Warning and Command System], lookdown shootdown interceptors, home-on-jam missiles, and nuclear armed missiles?

GENERAL CONFER. Yes. I think the ALCM has an excellent chance of penetrating these defenses since it has a very low cross-section and can fly at extremely low altitude making it difficult for the enemy radars to pick up.

SENATOR MCINTYRE. Then would you say that the cruise missile would be a significant hedge against a Soviet air defense system that would effectively counter the manned penetrating bomber?

GENERAL CONFER. Sir, it complements the manned bomber, but the bomber will still need to penetrate for the deeper target areas and the harder targets. The missile will complement the bomber in that it will soften the defenses and extend the strike capability. It can be utilized for some of the heavily defended areas' defense suppression to augment the bomber forces coming behind. Therefore, it is still our intent to go ahead and use the penetrating bomber as it was designed to penetrate the enemy defenses.[32]

30. *Report . . . on Authorizing Appropriations for Fiscal Year 1974 for Military Procurement, Research and Development, Construction Authorization for the Safeguard ABM, and Active Duty and Selected Reserve Strength, and for Other Purposes,* S. Rept. 93-385, 93 Cong. 1 sess. (1973), p. 28.

31. *Department of Defense Appropriations, 1975,* Hearings, pt. 4, p. 51.

32. *Fiscal Year 1975 Authorization for Military Procurement,* Hearings, pt. 7, p. 3726.

Because the air-launched cruise missile is in its early development phase, cost estimates are uncertain. The Air Force estimates an average procurement cost of $500,000 and a total development cost of $316 million.[33]

If a wide-bodied transport were to be used to launch the ALCMs, provisions would have to be made for missile-launching gear, precise navigation, and the required command and control equipment. We estimate that these modifications could be incorporated into a current wide-bodied transport at an average unit cost of $60 million with the expenditure of about $500 million for development. If it should prove desirable to increase aircraft hardness and flyout speed to improve prelaunch survivability in the ground alert mode, a new airframe would be required. In that case, we estimate that aircraft development costs would be $2 billion and unit procurement costs would be $65 million.

Air-Launched Ballistic Missiles

Little serious thought has been given to long-range air-launched ballistic missiles (ALBMs) since the Skybolt was canceled in the early 1960s. The Skybolt missile was intended for the late B-52 models then entering the force. It was conceived as a defense suppression weapon and as a way to extend the life of the manned bomber as air defenses improved. Skybolt was canceled because defense officials felt that bombers could penetrate air defenses without it, because of stiff competition from other weapons such as Minuteman, and because it was encountering cost overruns and schedule slippages.[34] But interest in ALBMs has recently been rekindled by the prospective decline in the survivability of Minuteman. This interest reached a high point in 1974 when the Air Force launched an obsolete Minuteman from a C-5 in a demonstration of the feasibility of air launching ICBMs.

In subsequent chapters we postulate air defenses that could make penetration by long-range cruise missiles difficult. In these cases, we equip the alternative bomber forces depending on long-range cruise missiles with enough ALBMs to suppress key air defense installations. We estimate that missiles with a range of 1,500–2,000 miles carrying ten Poseidon-like reentry vehicles would weigh between 45,000 and 50,000 pounds and that

33. Ibid., pp. 3694, 3726.
34. William W. Kaufman, *The McNamara Strategy* (Harper and Row, 1964), pp. 218–19.

it would cost $2 billion to develop such missiles and $20 million to procure each one.

By comparison, the Poseidon weighs about 65,000 pounds and can carry up to fourteen reentry vehicles. However, a missile incorporating more advanced technology and launched from high altitude in the direction of the target at the speed of the launching aircraft should be substantially smaller. Moreover, advances in guidance technology in the fifteen years since Skybolt was designed should make the development of a new ALBM a much less difficult process.

The Projected Program and Its Costs

Air Force planning for the bomber and tanker force is based on the following key premises:

—The B-1 bomber will be introduced into the force structure in fiscal year 1981 following a decision by the secretary of defense and the President to procure the aircraft in late calendar year 1975. Congressional approval for major procurement funding will be given during the spring and summer of 1976 in connection with the budget for fiscal year 1977. Major production contracts will be negotiated either in late 1976 or early 1977.

—The B-52G/H aircraft will be maintained through the 1980s. The Air Force estimates that the structural life of these aircraft will continue into the early to mid-1990s.[35]

—The remaining B-52D/Fs will be retained until the B-1 becomes available.

—The FB-111 will be operational for the next fifteen years.

—The active tanker force will be reduced with the transfer of 128 tankers to the Air Force Reserve. Eventually, a new cargo/tanker will be needed. Procurement of these new aircraft will be delayed until the B-1 program has been approved for production. Because of their shorter development cycle, however, the new aircraft could be operational at the same time as the B-1.

—The production line for the SRAM must be reopened to replace SRAM motors that will exceed their expected life by 1977 and to supply new missiles to arm the B-1.[36]

35. *Department of Defense Appropriations, 1975,* Hearings, pt. 4, p. 572.
36. "Report on the FY 1976 and Transition Budgets," p. II-38.

Table 3-3. Projected Number of Bombers, Tankers, and Air-to-Surface Missiles, Fiscal Years 1976–85[a]

Category	Fiscal year									
	1976	*1977*	*1978*	*1979*	*1980*	*1981*	*1982*	*1983*	*1984*	*1985*
Bombers										
B-52D/F	75	75	75	75	75	60	45	15	...	...
B-52G/H	255	255	255	255	255	255	255	255	255	255
FB-111	66	66	66	66	66	66	66	66	66	66
B-1	...	...	...	...	...	15	30	60	105	150
Tankers										
KC-135	480	480	480	480	480	465	450	420	390	360
Advanced	...	...	...	...	...	15	30	60	90	120
Air-to-surface missiles										
SRAM[b]	1,140	1,140	1,140	1,140	1,140	1,500	1,860	2,220	2,580	2,940
ALCM	...	...	...	...	...	...	...	360	720	1,080

a. Authors' estimates of equipment assigned to operational units. Estimates do not include aircraft procured to meet expected operating losses but not yet assigned to operational units.

b. There are currently 1,140 unit equipment SRAMs. See *Department of Defense Appropriations: Fiscal Year 1975*, Hearings before the Senate Committee on Appropriations, 93 Cong. 2 sess. (1974), pt. 1, p. 111. Twenty-four air-to-surface missiles are procured for each B-1.

—The ALCM will be deployed in the early 1980s for use in B-52 and B-1 bombers. The first flight of the missile is scheduled for 1978.[37]

Based on these premises, table 3-3 shows the structure of the planned U.S. bomber and tanker force for the next ten years. The estimated cost of acquiring and operating the projected bomber and tanker force is currently about $6 billion annually, but table 3-4 shows that these annual costs can be expected to increase to about $8 billion while the B-1 is being introduced into the force structure.

Several points in connection with table 3-4 require further explanation. Since the costs are given in constant fiscal year 1976 dollars, they do not reflect the potential effects of inflation. By applying the escalation factors recently adopted by the Office of the Assistant Secretary of Defense (Comptroller), we derived estimates of future costs in current dollars. The escalation factors decrease from about 8 percent in 1975 to less than 4 percent by 1980. The costs are shown as the total obligational authority, but the actual spending for each year may be different depending on the time lag between when Congress passes the appropriation bill and when the government actually pays for the goods or services. Ap-

37. Ibid., p. II-40.

Table 3-4. Projected Costs of the Bomber and Tanker Program, Fiscal Years 1976–85

Category						Fiscal year					
	1976	197T[a]	1977	1978	1979	1980	1981	1982	1983	1984	1985
	Millions of constant 1976 dollars										
Major system acquisition											
B-1	750	200	1,550	2,020	2,170	2,370	2,040	1,850	1,100	0	0
Advanced tanker	5	2	50	100	570	520	1,040	1,040	1,040	1,040	1,040
SRAM	3	2	35	210	210	210	210	420	420	420	420
ALCM	50	10	75	100	100	210	210	210	210	210	210
Other investment	1,260	320	1,260	1,260	1,260	1,260	1,260	1,260	1,260	1,260	1,260
Direct operating	1,600	400	1,600	1,600	1,600	1,600	1,610	1,640	1,700	1,780	1,940
Indirect operating	1,790	450	1,790	1,790	1,790	1,790	1,800	1,820	1,840	1,890	1,980
Total	5,460	1,380	6,460	7,080	7,700	7,960	8,170	8,240	7,570	6,600	6,850
	Millions of current dollars										
Total[b]	5,460	1,380	6,910	7,950	9,100	9,740	10,360	10,840	10,330	9,340	10,050

Sources: Authors' estimates based on data in various Department of Defense publications, in *The Budget of the United States Government, Fiscal Year 1976* (1975), and in testimony from hearings on the fiscal 1975 Defense Department budget before the Senate Armed Services and Appropriations committees. (See appendix A for a description of the costing methods.)
a. 197T is the designation for the three-month transition period from the end of fiscal 1976 on June 30, 1976, to the start of fiscal 1977 on October 1, 1976.
b. Figures are rounded.

pendix A contains a description of the cost categories and the methodology used in calculating the costs in table 3-4.

In the next two chapters we discuss two important elements of an effective bomber force—prelaunch survivability and the ability to penetrate enemy defenses—in order to set the stage for our examination of alternative means of modernizing the bomber force.

CHAPTER FOUR

BOMBER PRELAUNCH SURVIVABILITY

If, as we have concluded, the United States needs a strategic bomber force primarily as insurance against the failure or permanent degradation of the other components of the strategic retaliatory forces, U.S. bombers must be able to survive enemy attacks. One way to ensure bomber survivability is to put a portion of the force on airborne alert, making it essentially immune to attack. A second way is to maintain a portion of the force on ground alert so that it can be launched out from under an attack upon receipt of warning. The United States now depends on ground alert.

The U.S. bomber force relies heavily on two types of warning—strategic and tactical—for prelaunch survivability. Strategic warning would result when an assessment of all available information indicated that an attack was probable and that steps should be taken to enhance bomber prelaunch survivability. This judgment could be based on many indications—such as technical intelligence data on the state of adversary strike forces or evaluations of the political situation. The warning could occur hours, days, or even weeks before an eventual attack. Tactical warning, on the other hand, would be based on the detection of an actual attack launched against the bombers and their bases. Thus tactical warning would be measured in minutes. Tactical warning is essential if bombers on ground alert are to survive, even if their alert state has already been enhanced because of previous strategic warning.

Many government leaders and military strategists believe that in the current epoch nuclear war is extremely unlikely and that nuclear war unassociated with a desperate international crisis is almost totally implausible. Thus, in their view, strategic warning based on such a crisis is virtually certain. Those who hold this view, to be consistent, should be unwilling to see much money spent to hedge against the possibility of a surprise bolt-out-of-the-blue attack. Others fear that strategic warning

39

either will not be obtained or will not be acted upon because of misjudgments about the gravity of a situation or misinterpretations of indicators of the likelihood of war. Still others believe that a surprise attack is possible and that the United States should make substantial efforts to guard against this eventuality.

Some weapon systems, such as submarine-launched ballistic missiles (SLBMs), have an inherent capability, now and with foreseeable technology, to survive a surprise attack. Others, such as bombers, must be specially designed at potentially high cost to meet this objective. The following analysis suggests that it would be difficult to design and operate a bomber force to survive a severe surprise attack.

Airborne Alert

Bombers could be maintained in the air continuously or launched upon receipt of strategic warning. Once in the air, they would no longer depend on tactical warning and would be highly survivable, though the possibility of a successful attack against such aircraft cannot be completely ruled out. Not much has been written about ways to attack aircraft in flight at very long range, but it is clear that the problems in doing so would be formidable.

The primary problem would be to find ways to locate the aircraft, which could be anywhere in millions of square miles of airspace, at ranges of 3,000 to 5,000 nautical miles. Moreover, target aircraft would have to be discriminated from others. If this problem were solved, a mid-course air defense system could be deployed that would affect not only aircraft that use airborne alert for survivability but all bombers and tankers, once they were airborne.

In this study we consider airborne alert to be viable only for systems employing long-range missiles. Aircraft designed to penetrate enemy air defenses with large payloads at low altitude, such as the B-52 and the B-1, lack sufficient fuel reserves to permit an economical airborne alert. Thus large, efficient aircraft in the class of the Boeing 747 and the C-5 would be used on airborne alert. These aircraft have been optimized to achieve economic efficiency in air transport operations; this and their larger payloads make them suitable for airborne alert. For example, the largest of these aircraft, carrying up to about 135,000 pounds of missiles and missile-associated equipment (about fifty cruise missiles with ranges of about

1,500 nautical miles or three 45,000-pound ballistic missiles), and requiring refueling about once every eight to ten hours, could be supported in patrol areas with sufficient fuel at all times to fly forward to missile launch points and recover 1,000 nautical miles to neutral or friendly bases. One tanker per missile carrier could meet these refueling needs. In airline operations, Boeing 747s have been kept flying 50 percent of the time.[1] Thus rates somewhat in excess of this should be attainable in airborne alert operations. We use 60 percent in later parts of this study.

The acceptability of an airborne alert system hinges on other considerations, however—considerations that depend more on qualitative political judgments than on technical and military factors. Airborne alert patrol areas could no doubt be located over water or the arctic, but the possibility of accidents involving large numbers of nuclear weapons, perhaps fifty or more, would be of concern. Historical evidence suggests that airborne alerts would be infrequent and relatively short—a matter of days or at most weeks—and there would be less chance for accidents to occur during a short alert than during a prolonged one. The need for longer periods of airborne alert, perhaps measured in months, cannot be totally ruled out, however. In either case, there would also be the danger that accidents could occur during the takeoff or landing of aircraft laden with nuclear weapons going to or coming from patrol and could involve significant numbers of citizens and their property. Such possibilities could result in substantial opposition to airborne alert, depending on the public's perception of the gravity of the crisis.

Another important consideration in the use of airborne alert during a crisis is the effect this action could have on the crisis itself. Some would regard such a dramatic move as helping to stabilize the crisis; others would view it as a provocative act. In any case it is difficult to predict the outcome of such a step.

Ground Alert and the SLBM Threat

The sequence of events by which bombers on ground alert could achieve prelaunch survivability is, in essence, simple. If enemy missiles were launched against American bomber bases, they would be detected by U.S. warning systems, and bombers on ground alert could take off to escape

1. "Boeing 747 Operating and Cost Data: Third Quarter, 1973," *Aviation Week and Space Technology,* vol. 100 (February 18, 1974), p. 52.

the attack. After bombers are airborne and have attained safe flying speeds, they can fly in randomly selected directions away from their bases, creating an area of uncertainty in their location. Measured from the point at which safe flying speed is reached, this area is roughly a circle whose radius grows at the speed the bombers can fly. The probability that bombers will be destroyed by an attack, to a first approximation, can be obtained by calculating the ratio of the expected lethal area of the warheads used in the attack on a given base to the area of uncertainty in which the bombers from that base are located.

The most important aspects of the threat to bombers on ground alert are (1) the number of attacking missiles, (2) the time of flight of these missiles, (3) the yield of their warheads, and (4) the rate at which the attacking missiles are launched. Only submarine-launched missiles can seriously threaten the prelaunch survivability of U.S. strategic bombers on ground alert because only they can be launched at short range. Both ballistic missiles and cruise missiles when launched from submarines could pose such a threat.

Number of Attacking Missiles

The maximum number of SLBMs available to attack U.S. bomber bases depends primarily on the number of Soviet submarines and on Soviet patrol practices. U.S. defense officials suggest that current Soviet submarine deployments do not constitute a serious threat.[2] But since the Soviet Union could place more submarines in patrol areas close to U.S. coasts, this assessment might change.

The Interim Agreement[3] permits the Soviet Union to have 62 nuclear-powered submarines with 950 launchers. The new agreement reached at Vladivostok[4] would permit more, and as Soviet land-based intercontinental ballistic missiles (ICBMs) become less survivable the USSR may

2. *Fiscal Year 1975 Authorization for Military Procurement, Research and Development, and Active Duty, Selected Reserve and Civilian Personnel Strengths,* Hearings before the Senate Armed Services Committee, 93 Cong. 2 sess. (1974), pt. 7, pp. 3919–20; and "United States Military Posture for FY 1975," Statement by Admiral Thomas H. Moorer, USN, Chairman, Joint Chiefs of Staff, before the House Armed Services Committee (n.d.; processed), p. 62.

3. Interim Agreement between the United States and the Union of Soviet Socialist Republics on Certain Measures with Respect to the Limitation of Strategic Offensive Arms, signed at Moscow, May 26, 1972.

4. Joint Soviet-American Statement on Strategic Arms Limitation, November 24, 1974.

Table 4-1. Estimated Number of Soviet SLBMs That Could Be Kept on Station, Depending on Submarine Transit Speed and Size of Crew[a]

Transit speed[b] *(knots)*	*One crew per submarine*[c]		*Two crews per submarine*[d]	
	Submarines on station	*SLBMs on station*	*Submarines on station*	*SLBMs on station*
5	14	211	16	246
10	21	316	32	491
15	23	351	37	573
20	24	368	40	614

a. Assuming 948 SLBMs with 90 percent of the launchers available for patrol and an average of 15.3 launchers per submarine (based on estimate of forces given in text).
b. Transit speed is the average speed used to get to and from patrol areas.
c. Patrol duration 120 days and 1.5 patrols per ship per year.
d. Patrol duration 90 days and 3.5 patrols per ship per year. One crew would be at sea and one ashore.

deploy more. We based the ensuing analysis, however, on levels permitted by the Interim Agreement since they are ample to create a serious threat.

The Soviet Union now has thirty-four Yankee-class submarines. In addition it is constructing two types of Delta-class ships—one with twelve launchers and one with more launchers—we assume sixteen.[5] This could lead in time to the following submarine forces:

Class	*Number of submarines*	*Number of launchers on each submarine*	*Number of launchers in each class*
Yankee	34	16	544
Delta	11	12	132
Delta	17	16	272
Total	62	...	948

The Yankees are believed to be equipped with SS-N-6 missiles having a range of 1,300–1,600 nautical miles (nm) and the Deltas with 4,200-nm SS-N-8s.[6]

How long submarines remain on station in patrol areas depends in part on the lengths of the voyages to and from patrol areas and the number of crews (either one or two) provided for each submarine. The length of the voyage from Murmansk to waters just off the East Coast of the United States is about 3,600 nautical miles and from Vladivostok to the West Coast about 4,000 nautical miles. Table 4-1 shows the number of Soviet

5. "Report of Secretary of Defense James R. Schlesinger to Congress on the FY 1976 and Transition Budgets, FY 1977 Authorization Request and FY 1976–1980 Defense Programs" (February 1975; processed), p. II-14.
6. "United States Military Posture for FY 1976," Statement by General George S. Brown, USAF, Chairman, Joint Chiefs of Staff, before the Senate Armed Services Committee (n.d.; processed), pp. 20–23.

SLBMs that might be kept on station if the Soviet Union were to engage in close-in patrols. If the Soviet submarines were to transit at modest speeds, say 10 knots, they could keep about 300 SLBMs in patrol areas with one crew per ship or about 500 with two crews per ship. Higher speeds and longer patrols, which would keep crews at sea more than half the time, could increase these figures but would also increase the risk of detection. The Soviet Union might also temporarily increase patrol levels in anticipation of hostilities.

Flight Time of Attacking Missiles

The flight time of Soviet SLBMs can be estimated from knowledge of the range potential of the missiles and from the kinematics of ballistic trajectories. The SS-N-6 and SS-N-8 missiles, as indicated, have range capabilities of about 1,600 nmi and 4,200 nmi respectively. Because the center of the continental United States is only about 1,050 nautical miles from the coasts, these missiles would have excess energy if fired at far-inland bomber bases from patrol areas close to U.S. coasts. This energy could be used to shorten the time from launch point to target by flying the missiles on trajectories that are lower in altitude than minimum-energy trajectories for the same range—hence the term "depressed trajectories." A missile with a maximum range of 1,600 nm has the energy to fly 1,100 nm in about 530 seconds on a depressed trajectory compared with about 1,000 seconds on a minimum-energy trajectory. A missile with a maximum range of 4,200 nm has the energy to fly 1,100 nm in about 445 seconds on a depressed trajectory, and one with a maximum range of 5,500 nm might fly 1,100 nm in about 420 seconds;[7] minimum-energy flight times on maximum-range trajectories for these long-range missiles would be 1,500 and 1,800 seconds respectively. There is no evidence to suggest that the Soviet Union has tested its SLBMs in depressed trajectories;[8] it may be that Soviet missiles have serious shortcomings that preclude their use in this way. The possibility remains, however, that at some time in the future depressed trajectory missiles might figure importantly in the threat to U.S. bombers.

7. These are our own estimates, but the latter figure was used also by Captain James W. Winnefeld, USN, and Carl H. Builder in "ASW—Now or Never," *United States Naval Institute Proceedings*, vol. 97 (September 1971), p. 21.

8. *Fiscal Year 1975 Authorization for Military Procurement,* Hearings, pt. 7, p. 3916.

Warhead Yields of Soviet SLBMs

Private but authoritative sources place Soviet SLBM warhead yields in the megaton range.[9] Another source asserts that the SS-N-8 and SS-N-6 carry 1-megaton warheads.[10] The U.S. Poseidon missile reportedly can carry fourteen 50-kiloton warheads, which would have an explosive effect close to 2 megatons.[11] The SS-N-6 is apparently larger than the Polaris A-3, and the SS-N-8 larger than the Trident I missile.[12] It seems reasonable to expect Soviet SLBMs to have warhead yields of at least 1 megaton in the 1980s. Given Soviet propensities for larger warheads, the yields might be higher.

Rates of Fire of SLBMs

The rate at which SLBMs can be launched in an attack on bomber bases depends on the number of strategic ballistic missile submarines (SSBNs) conducting the attack and the rate at which each submarine can launch its missiles. Table 4-1 suggests that about twenty to thirty-three submarines might be involved, but this number would depend on Soviet patrol capabilities and whether Soviet SSBNs carried twelve or sixteen launchers.

No official data on Soviet launch rates are available to analysts. One source suggests one launch every fifteen seconds from each SSBN.[13] Because even higher launch rates would yield substantial benefits in an attack on U.S. bomber bases, it would seem prudent to consider the possibility that the USSR would design its weapon systems accordingly.[14] Moreover,

9. International Institute for Strategic Studies, *The Military Balance 1974–1975* (London: IISS, 1974), p. 73.

10. Robert L. Leggett, "Two Legs Do Not a Centipede Make," *Armed Forces Journal International,* vol. 112 (February 1975), p. 30.

11. See ibid.; Congressman Leggett puts the Poseidon warhead yield at 40 kilotons.

12. "United States Military Posture for FY 1976," chart 3, p. 21.

13. Winnefeld and Builder, "ASW—Now or Never," p. 21.

14. A capability to use depressed trajectory missiles in attacks on U.S. bomber bases is not likely to be a by-product of efforts to enhance Soviet retaliatory capabilities. Decisions would be needed to design missiles for depressed trajectories, to test them appropriately, to begin intensive routine close-in patrols (at great distances from Soviet ports), and to lay out war plans and procedures for their execution for the highly coordinated attack required. None of these efforts would be needed for attacks on anything but U.S. bomber bases. Should a program to acquire such a

U.S. bomber bases will be distributed in range, and if there were launch delays of several seconds between salvos during an attack, later salvos of missiles could be fired at the nearer bases, which would permit offsetting shorter times of flight. In our calculations we have assumed that all bases would come under attack at the same time.

Bomber Force Variables

The United States can manipulate five primary variables in an effort to attain adequate levels of prelaunch survivability. These are:
—Bomber reaction time.
—Bomber flyout speed and acceleration.
—Bomber hardness.
—The location of bomber bases.
—The number of bomber bases.[15]

Bomber Reaction Time

The single most important variable is the time required for the bombers to take off after missiles have been launched against bomber bases. Bomber reaction time depends on the quickness of the warning system, the state of alert of the crews, the design of the alert facilities and ramps for the bombers, and the capabilities of the bombers themselves.

Delays attributable to the warning systems are reported to amount to about 90 seconds.[16] This is the time it takes for a missile to climb into the upper reaches of the atmosphere and to be detected by U.S. warning satellites. Soviet sources put this time delay at sixty to ninety seconds.[17] Upon receipt of warning, crews would begin to scramble to their airplanes. The time it might take for this step would depend almost completely on the state of alert of the crews. It could be as little as two to four minutes if

---

specialized capability be undertaken, all measures, including high launch rates, which increase the prospect for success, would be fully justified.

15. We assume that the number of runways would be sufficient to avoid long queues of aircraft waiting to take off.

16. Barry Miller, "U.S. Moves to Upgrade Missile Warning Systems," *Aviation Week and Space Technology,* vol. 101 (December 2, 1974), pp. 16–17.

17. N. A. Lomov, ed., *Scientific-Technical Progress and the Revolution in Military Affairs: A Soviet View* (Moscow, 1973; translated and published by the U.S. Air Force, 1974), p. 57.

Table 4-2. Bomber Reaction-Time Budgets for Crisis and Day-to-Day Alerts
Seconds

Item	Crisis alert	Day-to-day alert
Warning delay	90	90
Time to scramble	0	120–240[a,b]
Engine start and taxi	30–60[a,c]	60[a]
Total time to brake release	120–150	270–390

a. Authors' estimates.
b. These figures are highly judgmental and potentially highly variable because they would depend mainly on the state of alert of the crews. In our judgment these estimates reflect a state of alert that would be difficult to maintain continuously for years.
c. Assuming, for the lower figure, that positioning planes at the ends of runways would eliminate taxi time, and for the higher figure, that pre-takeoff procedures would make it impossible to eliminate taxi time.

crews were essentially ready to fly, or many more minutes if they were in some lesser state of alert. If strategic warning had been obtained, they could be in the aircraft, thus eliminating scramble delays.

Once the crews were in the aircraft, preparation for takeoff could be initiated. The crews would start the engines and begin to taxi the bombers to the takeoff position. In bombers equipped with quick-start accessories, this might take as little as thirty seconds.[18] Another thirty seconds might be used taxiing to the runway—a delay that could be eliminated if the bombers were parked at the ends of runways.

One way to think of bomber reaction time is in terms of reaction-time budgets. Such budgets might be prepared for a crisis in which strategic warning would be obtained and for a surprise attack situation in which lower day-to-day alert states would apply. Table 4-2 shows such budgets.

Bomber Speed and Acceleration

It is important for bombers leaving their bases to rapidly create a large area of uncertainty as to their location. Thus the speed they can attain and the rapidity with which it can be attained have much to do with their survivability prospects.

We compare the acceleration of three kinds of bombers in figure 1:

—A "slow soft" aircraft, which has flyout speed and hardness, or resistance to nuclear effects, approximating that of a B-52 or a large widebodied transport such as the C-5 or the Boeing 747.

—A "soft high-acceleration" aircraft, which is the same conceptually

18. B-52s have quick-start accessories; the B-1s will have them, and any modern bomber could have.

Figure 4-1. Distance Flown by Fast Hard, Soft High-Acceleration, and Slow Soft Aircraft as a Function of Time after Brake Release

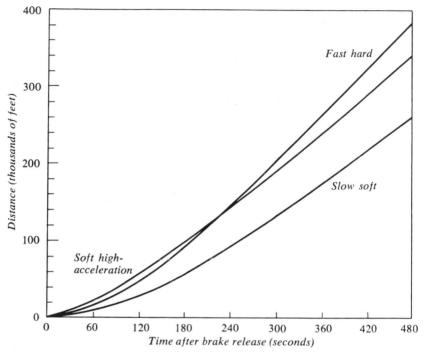

Source: **Authors'** estimates based on various unclassified data.

as the slow soft but obtains quick acceleration on takeoff by using rocket assistance. B-52s, wide-bodied aircraft, or B-1s could be equipped with rocket assistance.

—A "fast hard" aircraft, approximating the FB-111 or the B-1.

Figure 4-1 depicts the flyout curves for these three aircraft. As might be expected, the slow soft aircraft does least well in putting distance between itself and the base from which it takes off. With rocket assistance, however, the slow aircraft do much better and significantly narrow the difference between their getaway performance and that of fast hard aircraft such as the B-1.

Bomber Hardness

Very little data are available on the resistance, or hardness, of airplanes to nuclear effects. No unclassified data are available that are specifically pertinent to the hardness of the B-52, the B-1, or wide-bodied aircraft. Moreover, because full-scale tests of these aircraft are impractical, both the United States and the Soviet Union will remain uncertain of the true hardness of their bombers.

Estimating the hardness of airplanes is a complex matter. At least three nuclear effects could damage airplanes—thermal radiation, gusts, and overpressure. Electromagnetic pulse effects might also come into play. The vulnerability of airplanes to these effects depends on a number of factors —the direction from which the effects arrive, their duration and intensity, the speed of the aircraft, flight loads on the aircraft when the effects arrive, etc. The various parts of an airplane will respond differently to these effects. For example, plastic canopies and radomes would be affected in one way and metal parts in another. The mission an airplane must perform would also influence the amount of damage that it could tolerate. Thus a tanker might be able to tolerate some damage and still be able to refuel a bomber, whereas a bomber on a far more complex mission might be able to tolerate little or no damage.

With so many variables, so little empirical data to apply, and such complex theoretical problems in estimating aircraft hardness, one should be highly skeptical of all hardness estimates, especially high ones. On the other hand, the speeds at which airplanes can fly and the number of bases on which they are dispersed would be accurately known, and reaction times should be relatively certain, especially in crises where special alerting procedures are possible. Calculations that depend mainly on speed, dispersal, and reaction time estimates should thus be more reliable than those that depend more heavily on hardness estimates.

Parked aircraft were exposed to nuclear effects in the nuclear tests of the 1950s. The results of these tests along with hardness criteria for parked aircraft have been reported by the Defense Department. The data suggest that large aircraft of transport types are likely to receive light damage at 1 pound per square inch (psi) overpressure, moderate damage at 2 psi, and severe damage at 3 psi. Light damage would leave an aircraft flyable, but performance might be restricted. Either moderate or severe damage would make the aircraft unflyable.[19]

Aircraft in flight are unlikely to suffer as much damage, particularly at the moderate and severe levels, as parked aircraft. On the other hand, aircraft with complex missions, such as those intended to fly thousands

19. Samuel Glasstone, ed., *The Effects of Nuclear Weapons* (U.S. Department of Defense, 1964), p. 256.

of miles and then penetrate for distances of 1,000 miles to 2,000 miles while closely following the terrain at low altitude, do not tolerate much damage. Thus, plates buckled or torn loose, cracked windshields or radomes, or similar damage could inhibit or preclude success in such complex missions.

The B-1 reportedly has been designed specifically to increase its hardness. Undoubtedly some increases in hardness have been attained, but for reasons previously stated, the hardness of the B-1 as well as that of other candidate aircraft should be regarded as quite uncertain.

Considering all factors, we would be inclined to pick hardnesses of 1 psi or 2 psi for the slow soft and soft high-acceleration aircraft, leaning toward the higher figure if the aircraft does not have to penetrate at low altitude. For fast hard aircraft, we would pick 3 psi on no better ground than the intuitive one that tripling an acceptable damage level from about 1 psi to 3 psi (where severe damage occurred in the only tests for which results are available) seems like a substantial improvement. In subsequent analyses, however, we treat the hardness of the fast hard airplane as a variable, thereby allowing for the possibility of hardness up to 6 psi.

Location and Number of Bomber Bases

It seems clear that aircraft seriously threatened by SLBMs should be moved as far from coastlines as practical to maximize the flight time of the missiles to the bomber bases and to get the planes out of the potential depressed trajectory ranges of lower-performance missiles such as early versions of the SS-N-6. The most interior region in the United States, disregarding areas vulnerable to missiles launched from submarines in Hudson Bay and the Gulf of Mexico, is the area covered by North Dakota, South Dakota, and Minnesota.[20] The center of this region is about 1,050 nautical miles from the Atlantic and Pacific oceans. A system of bases would thus be needed in these states and in the adjacent portions of surrounding states to ensure survivability. There are only about five Air Force bases in this area now. Unless commercial or other airfields can be used for strategic bombers, a large base construction program is therefore implied if the United States is to have fifty or more interior bases.

20. If Soviet submarines operated routinely in the Gulf of Mexico and Hudson Bay, shorter ranges for the attack would be available with even shorter times of flight for depressed trajectory SLBMs. Hudson Bay can probably be denied to Soviet SSBNs, but the Gulf of Mexico is more doubtful. This factor is one more uncertainty that must be taken into account in judging the viability of ground alert.

The more bases there are, the smaller the size of an average attack on each of the bases would be. The scattering of alert aircraft from their main operating bases to dispersal sites (either military or commercial airfields or specially constructed satellite bases) has long been recognized as one of the ways to improve the prelaunch survivability of the bomber force.

We treat dispersal in the next section by first using equal dispersal levels of seventy-five bases for all three aircraft types. These bases are assumed to be in the interior, about 1,100 nautical miles from submarine launch areas. We then examine the effects of dispersal on each aircraft type and adjust dispersal levels, when it appears appropriate, to improve prelaunch survivability.

Survivability Prospects for Bombers on Ground Alert

The factors just discussed can be combined in a simple mathematical model to produce estimates of bomber prelaunch survivability. The model used in this study and more detailed (and more abstract) results of our calculations are given in appendix B, but it is useful to present the highlights of this analysis here.

In figure 4-2 we have plotted the probability of survival for the three aircraft types under attack by 300 1-megaton SLBMs flying 900-second minimum-energy trajectories and 420-second depressed trajectories.

If the SLBMs fly minimum-energy trajectories, all three aircraft types have good survivability expectations, with the fast hard aircraft marginally better than the other two. Substantial differences among the three aircraft types are apparent, however, if the SLBMs fly depressed trajectories. The advantages of greater speed and hardness, such as that possessed by the B-1, are clear. None of the aircraft types exhibit high survivability, say 80 percent or greater, if a depressed trajectory attack comes without strategic warning.

Before moving on to a more complete comparison of the three aircraft types, it might be helpful to explore the possibilities for creating a bomber force capable of surviving a surprise attack. The fast hard aircraft seem to have the best prospects for achieving this goal. Figure 4-3 shows the survivability rates for fast hard aircraft of hardnesses of up to 6 psi. At this high level of hardness, with a reaction time of 270 seconds—four and one-half minutes from SLBM launch to bomber brake release—about 75 percent of the alert bombers would survive; but this percentage is ex-

Figure 4-2. Survival Probability for Fast Hard, Soft High-Acceleration, and Slow Soft Aircraft Dispersed on 75 Bases and Attacked by 300 1-Megaton SLBMs[a]

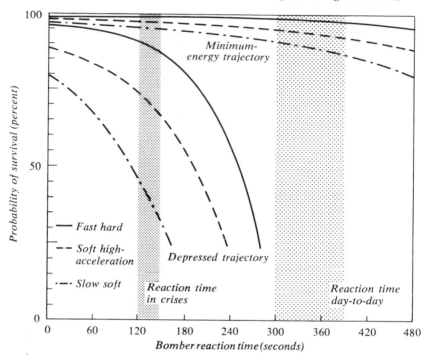

a. Hardness of soft aircraft is 1 psi and of hard aircraft, 3 psi. Depressed trajectory time is 420 seconds; minimum-energy trajectory time is 900 seconds.

tremely sensitive to increases in reaction time, and an additional delay of even half a minute would result in virtually all bombers being destroyed.

Figure 4-4 shows how additional dispersal would affect survivability if the reaction time were 270 seconds. Significant gains could be made by dispersing softer aircraft, but for harder aircraft (4 to 6 psi) dispersal levels above 100–125 bases would produce relatively small returns. Moreover, with day-to-day alert rates of 50–60 percent, only about 100–120 aircraft of a typical 200-aircraft force would be alert. Since dispersal bases *not* carrying alert aircraft could *not* be relied on to draw attacking weapons, there would appear to be at best only a weak case for dispersal on more than about 100 bases in the interest of surviving a *surprise* attack. It seems fair to conclude that only aircraft with a hardness of 4 psi or more have much promise of withstanding a surprise attack by depressed trajectory missiles if day-to-day reaction times are about 270 seconds. In

Figure 4-3. Effects of Hardness on the Survivability of Fast Hard Aircraft Dispersed on 75 Bases and Attacked by 300 1-Megaton SLBMs Flying Depressed Trajectories

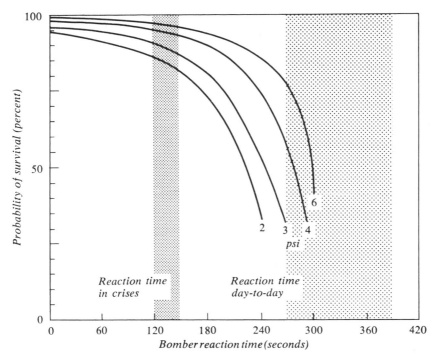

that case, the results are very sensitive to only small increases in reaction time.

Figure 4-5 shows similar curves for the three aircraft types at a reaction time of 150 seconds, which is the high side of the reaction time estimates if strategic warning is obtained. Two threat levels—300 and 500 SLBMs—are also shown. As was the case with an assumed reaction time of 270 seconds, the survivability of the fast hard aircraft is not very responsive to dispersal to more than about 100 bases. Gains can be obtained, however, by greater dispersal of the other two forces. Figure 4-5 also shows that for the fast hard and soft high-acceleration aircraft survivability is not particularly sensitive to the number of SLBMs in the attack. Thus we decided to examine in detail only the lower threat level.

If we apply a crisis alert rate of 85 percent to the current force of B-52G/Hs, somewhat over 200 aircraft would be on alert. A standoff missile carrier force might contain about 120 soft high-acceleration aircraft, each capable of carrying about 25 long-range cruise missiles. Of

Figure 4-4. Effects of Dispersal and Hardness on the Survivability of Fast Hard Aircraft Attacked by 300 1-Megaton SLBMs Flying Depressed Trajectories[a]

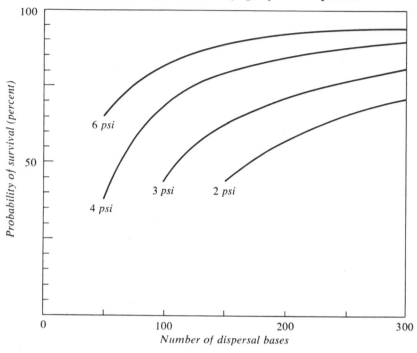

a. Reaction time is assumed to be 270 seconds.

these aircraft, about 100 might be alert. If the levels of dispersal for the two soft aircraft are increased to 200 and 100 interior bases, respectively, and to 100 interior bases for the fast hard aircraft, and if hardness uncertainties for the soft high-acceleration and fast hard aircraft are taken into account, the survivability estimates shown in figure 4-6 can be calculated.

Figure 4-6 shows how the survival prospects of these three forces would vary with reaction time and with hardness if they were attacked by 300 1-megaton SLBMs flying depressed trajectories. None of the forces do well without strategic warning, but all do at least moderately well with strategic warning. The fast hard aircraft is clearly superior, but not much over the soft high-acceleration plane. The slow soft airplane is clearly inferior but with strategic warning can produce survivability rates of 70 to 80 percent. It should be emphasized that these results depend heavily on the high dispersal levels used. If for political or other reasons the number of air bases cannot exceed, say, fifty bases for any of the options, the

Figure 4-5. Effects of Dispersal on the Survivability of the Three Aircraft Types Attacked by 300 and by 500 SLBMs Flying Depressed Trajectories[a]

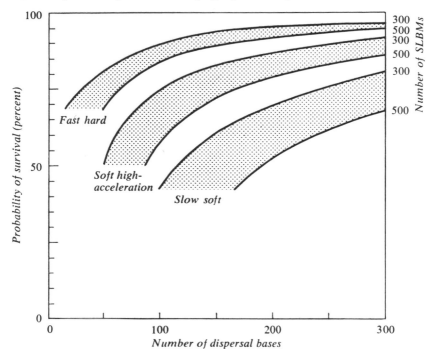

a. Hardness of soft aircraft is 1 psi and of hard aircraft, 3 psi. Reaction time is 150 seconds.

fast hard aircraft would be much more survivable than either of the soft aircraft. This becomes evident by reading the survivability prospects for the three aircraft types in figure 4-4 for fifty air bases. On the other hand, these analyses illustrate how dispersal can be used to compensate for lower aircraft hardness and speed.

Tanker Survivability

Two distinct cases must be dealt with in considering tanker prelaunch survivability. The first case is one in which bombers are capable without tanker support of accomplishing most, if not all, of their assigned missions. The second is when the reverse is true.

In the first case it would seem to be sufficient to maintain the tankers on alert *and* to place them on bases other than those on which the bombers

Figure 4-6. Survival Probabilities versus Reaction Time for the Three Aircraft Types with Different Dispersal Levels, Attacked by 300 1-Megaton Depressed Trajectory SLBMs

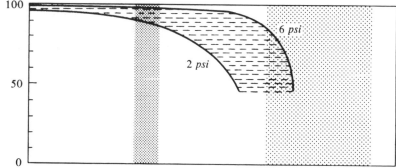

Fast hard aircraft, 100 dispersal bases

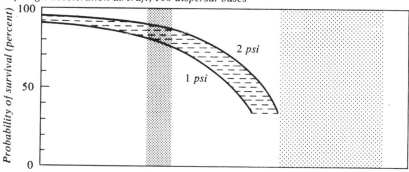

Soft high-acceleration aircraft, 100 dispersal bases

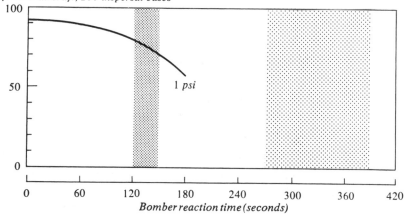

Soft slow aircraft, 200 dispersal bases

are located. Because the destruction of the tankers would not stop the bomber force, the tankers should be unattractive targets. In this situation the characteristics of the tankers would not need to be optimized for high survivability, though a high state of alert to make them hard to attack would be desirable.

In the second case, however, the tankers would be as important to the missions as the bombers themselves. Bomber effectiveness would depend on tanker survivability; thus the foregoing analysis of bomber-related issues would apply to tankers.

The B-52 and B-1 could both probably do much of the deterrent mission without tanker support. The FB-111 force, on the other hand, has far more marginal range capabilities and would probably need highly survivable tankers if given a central role in the future bomber force.

The Threat of Submarine-Launched Cruise Missiles

Most of our attention in this paper (and that of other analysts) has been focused on SLBM threats to bombers, but submarine-launched cruise missiles (SLCMs) could become threats as well. To be used against bomber bases, SLCMs would need certain specific characteristics. First, they would have to have enough range to get to interior air bases. Ranges of about 1,500 to 1,800 nautical miles would be sufficient to penetrate to Grand Forks, North Dakota, using even relatively circuitous routes. Second, the missiles would have to fly at very low altitudes—500 feet, for example—in order to avoid detection. Third, they would have to be able to fly a time-location profile to ensure arrival at all air bases at about the same time. The degree of simultaneity needed would depend on U.S. bomber reaction times, but the missiles probably would need to arrive within two to three minutes of each other—a degree of coordination that should be possible. Finally, the accuracy and yield of the missiles would have to be sufficient to provide relatively high confidence that bombers would be destroyed. Because bombers are relatively soft, even small warheads have large lethal radii; thus adequate accuracy would be easy to achieve if the Soviet Union acquires technology similar to that now available to the United States. As many as 75–100 cruise missiles with ranges of about 1,500 nm could be carried in the vertical launch tubes of a Polaris- or Yankee-class SSBN. Thus, only two or three submarines would need to be on station to launch enough missiles to attack up to about 100 air bases with two or more missiles.

The problems of obtaining tactical or strategic warning of a cruise missile attack are quite different from those associated with a ballistic missile attack, which would entail the use of perhaps twenty or thirty submarines. The United States would be far less likely to detect two or three submarines organizing for a cruise missile attack than twenty or thirty organizing for a ballistic missile attack. In addition, it is most unlikely that satellite warning sensors would detect the launch of cruise missiles because the trajectory could be kept low, well within the dense part of the atmosphere. Thus tactical warning would probably have to be obtained from detections of the cruise missiles during their flight of perhaps three hours. While this is a lot of time to make such detections, contiguous coverage of even relatively short perimeters would be difficult and expensive to obtain, especially since these air vehicles have small radar cross sections and would be flying at low altitudes. Moreover, flight routes for cruise missiles could be selected so that the missiles would fly over relatively isolated areas. Much of their routes could be in Canada if the U.S. bomber force were rebased in the north central portions of the United States, further complicating the tactical warning task.

Warning systems for a cruise missile attack might consist of airborne radars with lookdown capabilities or ground-based radars placed so as to give contiguous coverage around a collection of air bases or around individual air bases. Sufficient warning would have to be given to permit the bombers to take off and fly out of range of at least one weapon burst. Attacks on each base by several missiles could not, of course, be ruled out. Thus warning would be needed when the cruise missiles were at least four or five minutes from the air bases. Since the missiles could be flying perhaps 600 nautical miles per hour during this terminal phase of their missions, warning perimeters would have to extend out about forty to fifty nautical miles from the air bases. Warning systems with such capabilities have apparently not been given much attention, but it is clear that either airborne or ground-based warning systems for an SLCM threat would be expensive.

Arms Control Considerations and Bomber Prelaunch Survivability

Our analysis suggests at least two arms control measures that would help bomber force survivability: (1) a ban on testing depressed trajectory missiles; and (2) limits on areas where SSBNs are permitted to patrol, requiring Soviet SSBNs to stand off 1,000 to 1,500 nautical miles from U.S. borders, and vice versa. These measures would in effect prohibit SLBMs with very short times of flight.

Defense Department spokesmen suggest that a ban on testing depressed trajectory missiles is verifiable. They also believe that even if Soviet missiles now have some capability to fly depressed trajectories, two years of testing would be needed to verify this capability.[21] If Soviet missiles cannot fly on depressed trajectories, and if the Soviet Union pursues its usual conservative approach to new weapon developments, five years or more might be needed between the time a depressed trajectory missile is first tested and its widespread deployment, giving the United States substantial time to take countermeasures. A test ban would not interfere with the retaliatory capabilities of the SLBMs of the two sides since depressed trajectories are unnecessary for this purpose.

Limiting SSBN patrol areas would also be helpful because it would increase the range and hence the flight time of SLBMs to bomber bases. It is not clear whether such a limit could be verified, although proposals have been advanced to deploy antisubmarine warfare (ASW) forces to obtain warning of the close approach of Soviet SSBNs.[22] Defense Department spokesmen suggest that the United States could probably detect Soviet SSBNs organizing for an attack from close range.[23] If the U.S. mode of detection depends on the current noise levels of Soviet submarines, it can probably be relied on for years, since significant quieting of submarines usually requires major changes in their systems. Moreover, the Soviet SSBN force is relatively new and is unlikely to be replaced for many years.

Bomber survivability would be very important and SSBN patrol limits could become important if SSBN survivability should be undermined by ASW breakthroughs. Such breakthroughs depend on the ability to locate and track adversary SSBNs, and this ability by definition makes SSBN patrol limits verifiable. Patrol limits, even if negotiated before they are verifiable, would thus increase confidence in the bomber force as effective insurance against degradations in the SSBN force. Such limits would automatically offset an ASW breakthrough, at least in part.

Patrol area limits would have little or no effect on retaliatory capabili-

---

21. *Fiscal Year 1975 Authorization for Military Procurement*, Hearings, pt. 7, p. 3920.

22. Winnefeld and Builder, "ASW—Now or Never," p. 22.

23. *Fiscal Year 1975 Authorization for Military Procurement*, Hearings, pt. 7, p. 3920.

ties, particularly when long-range missiles such as the Trident I and the SS-N-8 are widely deployed. These missiles will be able to reach retaliatory targets using minimum-energy trajectories from ranges of 4,000 nm or more.

Patrol limits could interfere with the use of American forward SSBN bases at Rota, Spain, and at Holy Loch, Scotland, although these bases will decline in importance as longer-range missiles are deployed. Of course, patrol limits could be abrogated or violated quite suddenly; thus it would be unwise to depend too heavily on such a measure. On the other hand, the act of abrogation or violation would in itself constitute a hostile act and would justify offsetting actions by the other party. In any case, a limit would prohibit close-in patrols that might otherwise occur as a matter of course.

Agreement to and verification of limits would be complicated by attack submarines in the general purpose forces of the United States and the USSR and by submarines of third parties. It is probably difficult to distinguish SSBNs from other types of submarines, and banning the deployment of U.S. attack submarines in European waters might not be acceptable. Balancing these conflicting security interests would be necessary before patrol limits could be established. A ban on the testing and deployment of submarine-launched cruise missiles of the type and range that could threaten U.S. bomber bases from Soviet submarines would also add to bomber survivability if it could be effectively verified. But such a ban would raise other questions, some of which go beyond the scope of this study.

Summary

The threats from depressed trajectory SLBMs and cruise missiles treated in this chapter do not exist at present. The depressed trajectory SLBM threat, for instance, would require changes in Soviet SSBN patrol practices and the testing of Soviet missiles in depressed trajectory modes. The SS-N-8 may lack this capability; therefore new missiles may be needed for such a threat to materialize. Two to five years would be needed to obtain such a capability even if testing were to begin now.

Even with this capability, a well-coordinated operation by twenty to thirty SSBNs would be needed to attack the U.S. bomber force successfully. Virtually simultaneous initiation of the attack by all SSBNs would be of critical importance. Surprise would also be essential, and the testimony of Defense Department witnesses suggests that the United States could detect submarines organizing for such an attack. Moreover, a surprise attack seems highly implausible as long as any of the other U.S. strategic forces can retaliate.

The capabilities needed to attack bombers are not likely to be accidental by-products of Soviet forces designed for deterrence, since depressed trajectory missiles and close-in intensive patrols are not necessary to meet this objective. Close-in patrols, in fact, could easily compromise the survivability of Soviet SSBNs.

The use of cruise missiles against bomber bases—should the Soviet Union decide to develop this capability—would also entail great risks for the attacker. A cruise missile attack, like an SLBM attack, must be well-coordinated. Should such a threat develop, it could be nullified, at substantial but undefined expense, by suitable warning systems. The cruise missiles also might be detected accidentally early in their flight, thus assuring the survivability of alert bombers.

The outcome of even a well-coordinated attack on U.S. bomber bases is inherently uncertain. The margin between success and failure (viewed from either the Soviet or the U.S. perspective) is narrow. It requires only small deviations from expected reaction times, for example, to make large differences in outcomes, and other uncertainties are essentially unresolvable—aircraft hardness, for one.

There is no evidence that the Soviet Union is interested in either long-range SLCMs or depressed trajectory SLBMs. This fact, plus the difficulties associated with such capabilities and U.S. options to react in ways that could essentially nullify Soviet efforts, suggests that the early development of these threats is unlikely, although they could materialize eventually.

Although our analysis of the problems associated with bomber prelaunch survivability depends on approximations of the characteristics of the aircraft analyzed and a simplified model to characterize the complex interactions of SLBMs and bombers, we believe the following conclusions are justified:

1. High levels of bomber prelaunch survivability can be maintained by any of the aircraft considered in this study if depressed trajectory SLBMs and long-range submarine-launched cruise missiles are excluded from the threat.

2. If depressed trajectory missiles were to become a threat to the U.S. bomber force, major steps would need to be taken to protect the force.

a. If the United States depended on ground alert, the bomber force would have to be based on interior air bases.

b. Reaction times would have to be reduced to about two to three minutes against SLBMs with a flight time of 420 seconds to achieve high survivability levels. Slower missiles would permit second-for-second relaxation of these reaction time requirements. Increased airplane hardness, acceleration, and speed would also make slower reaction times tolerable.

c. The practicality of maintaining reaction times of two to three minutes day in, day out for years appears questionable. Day-to-day reaction times of four to seven minutes, though still fast, may be more sustainable. Unless reaction times of two to three minutes can be sustained, strategic warning would be needed by all aircraft considered (except for those with hardnesses of 4–6 psi) to permit the enhancement of their alert states and thus the reduction of their reaction times to a range of two to three minutes.

d. If these short reaction times are achieved, survivability prospects for fast hard aircraft against an SLBM attack are good, but their survivability is then not especially sensitive to aircraft hardness or to high dispersal levels. If the soft aircraft, even the unmodified B-52s, are sufficiently dispersed, they can attain good survivability levels, too, but as many as 100 to 200 air bases might be needed by soft aircraft.

e. Airborne alert is an alternative to ground alert; as a practical matter, though, strategic warning would be needed to initiate it, since airplanes on airborne alert would not be dependent on tactical warning. Aircraft with larger payload and fuel capacities are better suited for airborne alert than the B-52 and B-1.

3. If the USSR should eventually deploy long-range SLCMs, it would be necessary for the United States to develop suitable warning systems or to rely more extensively on airborne alert for survival.

CHAPTER FIVE

PENETRATION OF ENEMY AIR DEFENSES

In addition to achieving survivability, the U.S. bomber force must also be able to penetrate through Soviet air defenses to accomplish its retaliatory task. In this chapter, therefore, we address the main considerations in bomber penetration and examine alternative approaches to dealing with strategic air defenses.

Soviet Air Defenses

The Soviet Union currently maintains the most extensive strategic air defense system in the world. As noted earlier, the Soviet Union has about 2,600 active air defense interceptors supported by about 4,000 radars located at numerous early warning and ground control intercept sites. These long-range systems make up the area defenses of the Soviet Union, but there are also about 12,000 surface-to-air (SAM) launchers—short-range missile systems that provide so-called terminal, or close-in, defense of cities and other important targets. Some of the SAMs are placed in barriers along Soviet borders where they might intercept bombers entering the Soviet Union.[1]

During the past ten years Soviet interceptor forces have been declining by about 100 interceptors per year as older aircraft, such as MIG-17s and MIG-19s armed with guns, have been replaced with more advanced missile-armed interceptors such as the MIG-25 (the well-publicized FOX-BAT) and the SU-15. The MIG-23, a "swing wing" fighter armed with four air-to-air missiles and a gun may also serve in a future air defense role. U.S. defense officials expect the Soviet Union to deploy a new inter-

1. Data in this summary are drawn from "United States Military Posture for FY 1976," Statement by General George S. Brown, USAF, Chairman, Joint Chiefs of Staff, before the Senate Armed Services Committee (n.d.; processed), pp. 41–42.

ceptor near the end of this decade. However, General George S. Brown, chairman of the Joint Chiefs of Staff, has reported that the Soviet Union has not "demonstrated the capability of developing a radar capable of detecting and tracking from high altitude a bomber at low altitude against a background of signals reflecting from the ground." In his view this imposes a "fundamental constraint on Soviet interceptors' effectiveness against low-altitude bombers."[2]

The Soviet SA-2 is the most numerous Soviet strategic SAM. It was first deployed in 1958 and has been modernized and modified since then to improve its range and low-altitude performance. The SA-2 deployment is supplemented with smaller deployments of SA-3s, which were first introduced in 1961. These missiles are credited with the capability to intercept attacking aircraft "at low altitudes within a limited range of the launch site." Since 1967 the USSR has also been deploying the SA-5, the so-called Tallinn system, which at one time some authorities feared might possess both air defense and antiballistic missile (ABM) capabilities. A much older system, the SA-1, first deployed in 1954, is still active. For field army defense, the Soviet Union has developed and deployed the SA-6, a highly mobile SAM. This SAM, "employed with notable effectiveness in the recent [1973] Middle East hostilities, has impressive capabilities, particularly in dealing with low-altitude attacks."[3] Although SA-6s could be used for strategic defense, they have not appeared in this role.

Soviet air defense warning and control radars are at fixed sites except for the radars in MOSS aircraft. This system, the first Soviet attempt at an airborne warning and control system, "has worked in overwater exercises, but is unequal to the more challenging overland [detection and tracking] task."[4]

General Brown assessed the overall capability of Soviet air defenses as follows:

Despite the size of the Soviet air defense force and the projected improvements, there exists major weakness in low-altitude defense against penetrating bombers and in defense against the U.S. short-range attack missile (SRAM).[5]

There is other evidence to support this assessment. For example:

—The SA-2 was deployed extensively in North Vietnam and opposed U.S. tactical and strategic aircraft there. The North Vietnamese inflicted

2. Ibid., pp. 43, 45.
3. Ibid., p. 45.
4. Ibid., p. 46. MOSS is the code name used by the North Atlantic Treaty Organization for this system.
5. Ibid., p. 45.

about 3 percent attrition on U.S. B-52s over Hanoi during the bombing raids of late 1972. The SA-2 was *much less* successful against tactical aircraft such as F-4s. U.S. aircraft were not exposed to a significant interceptor threat in Vietnam.

—The SA-6 was used by the Egyptians during the conflict in the Middle East in October 1973. Israeli loss rates of A-4s, the aircraft relied on most heavily to attack ground targets and therefore probably most frequently exposed to low-altitude missiles, appear to have been between 10 and 15 losses per 1,000 sorties, or 1 percent to 1.5 percent.[6]

—An estimate, attributed to the Air Force, put the probability of U.S. strategic bomber penetration of the Soviet Union in a nuclear war at 85 percent.[7]

—In testimony before a Senate subcommittee, both Navy and Air Force witnesses expressed the view that low-altitude subsonic cruise missiles could penetrate existing Soviet air defenses at low altitude.[8]

—Secretary of Defense Schlesinger testified in early 1975 that "without a 'lookdown, shootdown' capability, the Soviet air defense interceptor aircraft are not likely to offer a serious obstacle to our bomber force."[9]

Another deficiency of Soviet air defenses is their vulnerability to ballistic missile attack. The SAMs and their warning and control elements are fixed, soft, and undefended by antiballistic missile defenses. The air defenses themselves lack the capability to intercept strategic ballistic missile reentry vehicles. Thus attacks on selected air defense sites would destroy the sites and could seriously degrade both the area and terminal defenses. (It would not, of course, be necessary to suppress all elements of the air defense system.) Moreover, for a period of unlimited duration the ABM treaty prohibits giving SAMs an ABM capability or deploying enough ABMs to protect the air defenses.[10] This prohibition is reinforced by a ban on testing systems, other than ABM systems, in an ABM mode.

6. William D. White, *U.S. Tactical Air Power: Missions, Forces, and Costs* (Brookings Institution, 1974), p. 70.

7. Michael Getler, *Washington Post,* December 15, 1974.

8. *Fiscal Year 1975 Authorization for Military Procurement, Research and Development, and Active Duty, Selected Reserve and Civilian Personnel Strengths,* Hearings before the Senate Armed Services Committee, 93 Cong. 2 sess. (1974), pt. 7, pp. 3661, 3701–2.

9. "Report of Secretary of Defense James R. Schlesinger to the Congress on the FY 1976 and Transition Budgets, FY 1977 Authorization Request and FY 1976–1980 Defense Programs" (February 1975; processed), p. II-16.

10. Treaty between the United States and the Union of Soviet Socialist Republics on the Limitation of Anti-Ballistic Missile Systems, signed at Moscow, May 26, 1972.

In sum, it seems fair to conclude:

—Current Soviet air defenses have little capability at low altitude to intercept bombers or subsonic cruise missiles and have no capability to intercept SRAMs once they are launched.

—Soviet air defenses are vulnerable to ballistic missile attack and will remain so as long as the ABM treaty is effective.

Is There an Air Defense Penetration Problem?

It would be time-consuming and expensive for the Soviet Union to correct the most serious shortcomings in its air defense system. Even if it could make its air defense system invulnerable to ballistic missile attack and make penetration with winged vehicles difficult and more costly for the United States, the system could still be *bypassed* by modern air-launched ballistic missiles flown from outside air defense perimeters. Only ABM-capable air defenses or ABMs could attack such weapons successfully; air defenses with ABM capability, however, are banned, and only 100 ABM interceptors are permitted by the ABM treaty. It would appear, therefore, that Soviet air defenses can be penetrated with impunity by air-launched strategic ballistic missiles (ALBMs).

The United States could design a bomber force that relied entirely on ALBMs. To deliver 400 1-megaton equivalents after strategic warning, this force might consist of about 145 aircraft, each carrying three ballistic missiles weighing about 45,000 pounds and carrying ten Poseidon-like 50-kiloton reentry vehicles. Should the threat to the prelaunch survivability of ground alert aircraft necessitate airborne alert during crises, a force of about 185 missile carriers with 185 supporting tankers could deliver about 400 1-megaton equivalents.

ALBMs carrying multiple independently targetable reentry vehicles (MIRVs) would come under the limit of 1,320 MIRV-equipped missiles set at Vladivostok.[11] Thus intercontinental ballistic missiles (ICBMs) or submarine-launched ballistic missiles (SLBMs) with MIRVs would have to be dismantled or replaced with missiles lacking MIRVs to make room under the limits for the ALBMs. It seems likely, though, that at some future time the United States might want to move missiles with MIRVs

11. Joint Soviet-American Statement on Strategic Arms Limitation, November 24, 1974.

out of ICBM silos to more survivable basing modes. Bombers offer such a possibility. The ICBM silos from which the MIRV-carrying missiles would have to be removed could be dismantled or their missiles could be equipped with large single reentry vehicles. These reentry vehicles would provide the accurate high-yield capability that is now attributed to the bomber force.

While ICBMs would be less survivable than bombers (under the presumption that a threat to silos has emerged), they would have better penetration capability and could get to targets much faster. Thus they would be better suited for the limited strikes that would be most likely to occur in the initial stages of a war before large attacks were carried out. Moreover, ALBMs would reduce some of the most serious problems with which the bomber force would be faced in attacks on military targets and attacks limited to a few weapons. The time of flight would be substantially reduced since much of the trip from airplane patrol areas (or air bases) to the target would be at ballistic velocities of thousands of miles per hour, and individual missiles could be used that would have a high penetration probability.

We turn now to issues associated with bomber forces that would not depend primarily on ALBMs.

The Question of "Mutual Support"

The current and prospective inadequacies of Soviet air defenses against strategic ballistic missiles present the United States with the possibility of using ICBMs and SLBMs to suppress air defenses to aid bomber penetration. Though defense suppression may not be important now because of the inadequacies of Soviet air defenses at low altitude, improved air defenses might change this. Then defense suppression by ballistic missiles might be more attractive; it should be especially effective against advanced-technology SAMs deployed near cities or other targets for close-in terminal defense. For example, 200–400 Poseidon and Trident reentry vehicles of about 7,400 now planned for deployment (about 4,000 would be at sea and hence survivable) might destroy enough SAM sites to enable easy penetration by large numbers of higher-yield cruise missiles. Alternatively, the ballistic missiles could attack the targets directly, relieving the bombers of the task of destroying targets with tough terminal air defenses. Ballistic missiles could also be used to attack interceptor bases and bases for airborne warning and control systems (AWACS). Though the interceptors and AWACS might not be caught on the ground, the destruction of their primary bases and probable dispersal bases could grossly disrupt the performance of these forces some hours later when U.S. bombers arrive.

Significant economic efficiencies in U.S. bomber forces could be realized if reliance on ballistic missile suppression of air defenses were part of the policy framework for procuring bombers. For example, under such a policy there would be little or no need for U.S. bombers to fly into the Soviet Union since cruise missiles could be fired from outside Soviet borders to attack even terminally defended targets after SAM suppression by ballistic reentry vehicles.

The argument against this policy is that it would make the bomber force potentially dependent, at least in part, on the missile force. This dependence in turn would reduce the extent to which the bomber force ensures against the failure of the missile force.

The position of the Defense Department on this matter is somewhat ambiguous. In 1975 Secretary of Defense Schlesinger testified as follows:

Each leg of the triad is not required to retain independently a capacity to inflict in a second strike unacceptable damage upon an attacker. Instead, the three legs of the triad are designed to be mutually supporting.[12]

Later in the same testimony, he explained:

Missiles, for example, could help clear the way for bomber penetration, and bombers, in turn, could help to fill the gap of those important targets missed by missiles.

It is this mutually supporting deterrent capability, in addition to the reasons I enumerated last year [1974], that strongly commends to us the continued retention in our strategic forces of both ICBMs and bombers as well as SLBMs.[13]

Schlesinger had expressed similar views on other occasions—for example, at the B-1 "rollout" ceremony.

This nation has long maintained a triad of strategic forces: the bombers, the ICBMs and SLBMs. Today we maintain the triad, *not because each leg of the triad must independently retain the capacity to strike back after an initial attack and inflict unacceptable damage on an attacker.* Overall, the forces must, of course, retain that capability—*with each component contributing to and mutually supporting achievement of the larger objective of deterrence.*[14] (Emphasis added.)

The secretary's views seemed clear—mutual support and, specifically,

---

12. "Report on the FY 1976 and Transition Budgets," p. I-14.
13. Ibid., p. II-20.
14. Department of Defense News Release 508-74, October 26, 1974, pp. 1–2.

ballistic missile suppression of air defenses apparently were part of his policy framework. Other Defense Department spokesmen, however, have presented contrasting points of view. For example, E. C. Aldridge, Jr., deputy assistant secretary of defense (strategic programs), stated that

one of the purposes of the bomber force is to hedge against ballistic missile failure. It would therefore seem illogical to design a bomber force which was dependent on ballistic missile success to suppress an air defense system to insure success of the bomber force.[15]

The bomber force is evidently being designed in line with this latter view: to be able to carry out the retaliatory mission without support from the ballistic missile forces.

We believe that, in buying its bomber force, the United States can safely assume that ballistic missiles can be used to suppress air defenses as long as the prospects for SLBM survivability remain unchanged and as long as an *effective mobile (and hence difficult to target) SAM defense* against strategic cruise missiles is not deployed. In the analysis that follows, however, we include in alternative bomber forces those capabilities needed to retaliate independently. This is an analytic device to ensure a maximum degree of comparability between competing forces, one of which is the B-1 force recommended by the Defense Department.

The Role of Electronic Countermeasures

Electronic countermeasures (ECM) equipment on bombers or missiles can be used to interfere with the performance of air defense radars, communications links, and other defensive electronic equipment. For example, ECM equipment can jam enemy radars with electronic noise, thereby denying range measurements to the radars; can create targets where there are none; and can generate signals that disrupt radar antenna-tracking subsystems.

The defenses can employ electronic counter-countermeasures (ECCM) that can reduce the effectiveness of ECM, even nullifying it completely in some cases. Nonelectronic devices can also be employed against ECM; for example, in North Vietnam, optical tracking equipment was installed on SA-2 SAM radars to counteract U.S. ECM, which evidently was interfering with SA-2 radar-tracking capabilities. Various sorts of data processing and tactics can also help to overcome ECM.

15. "Statement of E. C. Aldridge, Jr. . . . before the House Armed Services Committee on the U.S. Strategic Bomber Force" (April 1975; processed), p. 5.

To a substantial degree, the effectiveness of ECM depends on knowledge of the adversary's electronic equipment—antenna patterns, radar frequencies, the ability to change frequencies or use unexpected frequencies, data processing ability, and tactics. In conventional warfare, where many sorties are flown against defensive systems and where, so far, initial attrition rates have been at most a few percent, there is time for both the offense and defense to learn and adjust. Even new ECM and ECCM equipment can be developed and introduced, as it was in Vietnam. In strategic nuclear war, where offenses and defenses are likely to be exposed to each other just once over a brief period, the effectiveness of ECM would depend much more on prewar knowledge of the characteristics of the defenses.

If the existence of highly effective air defenses (much more effective than any yet deployed by anyone) is presupposed, a situation is created in which reliance on ECM is roughly equivalent to basing the effectiveness of the bomber force on prewar knowledge of the electronic characteristics of these good air defenses. Many of these characteristics—for example, internal data processing characteristics—may be unobservable by technical intelligence collection. Inadequate ECM could conceivably result in catastrophic inadequacies in the bomber force. This possibility was suggested by Malcolm R. Currie, director of Defense Research and Engineering in the Department of Defense, in his testimony before a Senate committee.

The ECM suites for both the B-52 and the B-1 were shown to be effective [in the Joint Strategic Bomber Study], but the *extreme sensitivity* of the performance of the penetrating bomber to the quality of its ECM was manifest. This sensitivity is *so crucial* that continuous reevaluation of ECM interactions are called for over the long term. Furthermore, we believe viable alternatives to the penetrating bomber must be pursued. Our cruise missile programs . . . constitute such an alternative, and we are searching for others.[16] (Emphasis added.)

The difficulties are further illustrated by the Joint Strategic Bomber Study of the Department of Defense. Evidently the department assumed that the Soviet AWACS could not be jammed (it had previously given assurances that the U.S. AWACS could not be significantly degraded in defensive operations by Soviet ECM) but did assume that Soviet look-

16. "The Department of Defense Program of Research, Development, Test and Evaluation, FY 1976," Statement by Dr. Malcolm R. Currie, Director of Defense Research and Engineering before the Senate Appropriations Committee, 94 Cong. 1 sess. (February 26, 1975; processed), pp. V-17–18.

down, shoot down fighters and air-to-air missiles could be. In short, the study permitted hypothetical advanced high-performance interceptors to be vectored to penetrating bombers before any effective countermeasures were applied.[17] Then the Defense Department was able to assure itself that it could deal with advanced Soviet fighters using ECM.

The issue is whether or not to assume that ECM will work in planning and *procuring* the bomber force. Since most ECM equipment does not displace weapons (decoys being the main exception to this generalization), an assumption that ECM will work as intended, producing relatively high penetration probabilities—80 percent, for example—would result in procuring smaller and less expensive U.S. bomber forces. Only about seventy-seven alert B-1-type bombers would be needed to deliver the equivalent of 400 1-megaton bombs if the penetration probability were 80 percent. Under similar circumstances and without prelaunch attrition, the 210 B-1s planned by the Air Force could deliver about 670 1-megaton equivalents in about 2,000 air-to-surface missiles (ASMs) from a 60 percent alert rate and almost 950 in about 2,800 ASMs from an 85 percent alert rate. If about one-tenth of the alert airplanes were destroyed before launch, the equivalent yields would be reduced to about 600 megatons and 850 megatons respectively, still 1.5 to 2.1 times the task defined in chapter 2. These estimates illustrate Defense Department ambiguity on the question of *relying* on ECM for force planning purposes.

On the one hand, Dr. Currie has testified:

Bomber penetrativity against advanced fighters (having look-down shoot-down capability) depends most on ECM effectiveness.[18]

On the other hand, the department supports a B-1 force (and retention of B-52s) that is much larger than needed if ECM works as expected. In other words, the Defense Department says it is relying on ECM but appears to be buying forces on a scale that could be best justified if ECM does not work.

We believe there are too many uncertainties and unresolvable questions about the effectiveness of ECM to rely on it in buying bomber forces. We

17. These observations were made by Senator Thomas J. McIntyre of New Hampshire in a letter to Secretary Schlesinger, March 14, 1975, and in the response of W. J. Clements, Jr., deputy secretary of defense, to Senator McIntyre, April 9, 1975. The Joint Strategic Bomber Study itself is a classified document.

18. "The Department of Defense Program of Research, Development, Test and Evaluation, FY 1976," p. V-15.

think there should be an investment in ECM, of course, to gain higher confidence in the bomber force and to try to stretch deployed forces further, but we also think the size of the force should be based on the assumption that only high-confidence penetration aids will work against future hypothetical, and hence unknown, air defenses. In the analyses that follow, no credit is taken for ECM (except as ECM is embodied in armed decoys for the penetrating bombers, the B-52 and B-1).

Projected Soviet Developments and Possible U.S. Reactions

The Soviet Union has not displayed the types of systems we will discuss here, although such systems may be under development in Soviet laboratories. In some instances, we have no better basis for postulating the development of these high-performance air defense components than that such developments would be logical in light of U.S. bomber capabilities and of other Soviet air defense undertakings. These Soviet air defense components are thus hypothetical, and our mental images of the devices therefore stem from similar systems the United States has or is developing.

Our discussion of U.S. reactions to such developments is substantially less hypothetical. There is little or no doubt that the kinds of offensive weapons envisioned could be built. Long-range cruise missiles, armed decoys, and air-launched ballistic missiles are all reasonably well-defined, and all are clearly within the technological grasp of the United States. Long-range cruise missiles are already being developed and all the subsystems have been demonstrated. As Dr. Currie noted, long-range cruise missiles are a viable alternative to the penetrating bomber. The SRAM has already been deployed, and its performance in most respects is not in doubt. The B-1 airplane (but not the B-1 weapon system) and the soft missile carriers exist, at least as operational commercial or military airplanes. The "fast hard" missile carrier is conceptually a much simplified subsonic version of the B-1.

When we undertook the quantitative analyses, we employed simple models that we believed would yield fair *relative* estimates of force performance. But the absolute accuracy of our simple models as well as the accuracy of far more complicated ones is suspect, since none of the models has been (and we hope never will be) tested against the results of the large-scale nuclear air battles the models attempt to characterize.

Soviet Deployment of AWACS and Lookdown,
Shootdown Interceptors

The development of airborne warning and control systems and interceptors that can look down and missiles that can shoot down against
background clutter is a difficult technical task. But the development and
deployment of such equipment by the USSR would give their major air
defense components the capability to detect, track, and attack low-flying
U.S. bombers with interceptors under close control, that is, with interceptors vectored to the bombers by the AWACS with high probabilities
that the vectoring would result in interceptor detection of the bomber. In
its extreme form, this capability would permit air battle management by
the defense over a wide area in which interceptor forces could be brought
to bear in a near optimal way against penetrators in that area. With this
good control, the capabilities of the air defenses would be maximized, and
the defense would be able to exhaust its firepower on the attacking bomber
force. In subsequent analyses, we assume the existence of such control
capabilities.

It is useful to suggest in familiar terms what these air defense forces
might consist of. The U.S. F-14 carries six Phoenix missiles. If, for example, each missile had an overall kill probability of 50 percent and if
each were fired at a separate target, a Soviet F-14-type aircraft supported
by an appropriate number of Soviet AWACS and faced with hundreds of
penetrators might have such good control and a wealth of interception
opportunities. Thus 1,000 intercepts would imply 333 F 14 type aircraft
actually getting into the air battle. If some of the interceptors were mal-
deployed, some not on alert, and some out of commission and unreliable,
the force of F-14-type aircraft required to make 1,000 intercepts might
easily reach 500 to 600. The number of supporting AWACS is harder to
estimate, but at one time the United States envisioned the procurement of
more than twenty-five such airplanes for U.S. continental air defenses.[19]
Since Soviet territory is even larger, forty to fifty AWACS might be required for Soviet area defense forces. The investment cost of an air defense
system consisting of 40 to 50 AWACS and 250 to 300 F-14s could easily
amount to $10 billion if deployed by the United States.

19. *Fiscal Year 1974 Authorization for Military Procurement, Research and De-*
velopment, Construction Authorization for the Safeguard ABM, and Active Duty
and Selected Reserve Strengths, Hearings before the Senate Armed Services Committee, 93 Cong. 2 sess. (1973), pt. 6, p. 4628.

A penetrating bomber force with its large aircraft penetrating in relatively small numbers would be more vulnerable to this development than an air-launched cruise missile (ALCM) force, which would contain about 1,200 reliable ALCMs just to deliver 400 1-megaton equivalents, but the bombers would be able to take a number of steps to reduce their vulnerability to AWACS and lookdown, shootdown fighters. They could employ electronic countermeasures to deny information to the air defenses and to confuse and saturate them. The bombers could also attack with missiles capable of being guided to the AWACS. Like ECM, these techniques, however, are dependent on Soviet anti-ECM techniques and on the self-defense capabilities of Soviet AWACS. Because of this, their effects are uncertain. To gain higher confidence in the penetrating bomber force, the United States might equip the bombers with decoys. If the decoys themselves were armed with nuclear weapons, the offense could then inflict some minimum level of damage on the defense, even if the defense discriminated the decoys from the bombers and attacked the bombers first. Thus armed decoys would be more reliable than ECM in ensuring the effectiveness of manned bombers penetrating high-performance air defenses. An armed decoy would be little more than a long-range cruise missile equipped with electronics suitable for it to simulate a bomber to Soviet air defenses.

The number of decoys that might be needed would depend on the size and quality of the air defense and on the size and nature of the bomber force. For example, if an air defense system were of such high quality that it could always shoot down some specified number of penetrators— for example, 200—then a B-1 force, designed to minimize the number of bombers needed, attacking through such an air defense to deliver 400 1-megaton equivalents in SRAMs, would carry about six decoys per bomber. An alert surviving force of about 117 airplanes could do the task. The penetration probability would be about 70 percent. About 1,200 SRAMs would be delivered to targets. If the decoys were to fail as decoys and the defense were to attack the bombers preferentially, destroying all of them and some of the decoys, about 483 decoys containing about 166 1-megaton equivalents would penetrate to their targets. Thus the offense could enforce this minimum result for that level of defense capabilities. Tables 5-1 through 5-3 illustrate the effects on bomber force size and force loading of various levels of area air defense effectiveness.

In three ways, the cruise missile systems would be the least sensitive to the development of such air defense threats. First, a given number of

Table 5-1. Unmodified B-52s Required to Deliver 1,200 SRAMs to Targets against Area Defenses of Different Effectiveness[a]

Number of kills area defense can enforce	Alert surviving bombers required to deliver 1,200 SRAMs	Decoys per bomber	Delivery of 1-megaton equivalents offense can enforce
0	74	0.0	400
200	139	5.0	168
400	175	6.6	238
600	205	7.7	297
800	232	8.4	340
1,000	257	8.9	373

a. Assuming 20 SRAM and decoy spaces per unmodified B-52, no prelaunch attrition, and bomber and missile reliabilities of 90 percent each. SRAMs and decoys each carry 200-kiloton warheads. Bombs carried by B-52s or other bomber aircraft were not taken into account. To do so would reduce the number of aircraft required. The mathematical model on which this table is based appears in appendix C. For each threat level, we selected a number of decoys per bomber that minimizes the number of bombers needed to deliver 1,200 reliable SRAMs. In the model we assumed that the defense could enforce the number of kills shown in the first column, regardless of the number of penetrators (bombers plus decoys), providing only that the number of penetrators entering the air defenses would exceed the number of kills.

cruise missile carriers could tolerate a higher level of area defense. For example, if the defense could enforce 1,000 kills on the offense, about 151 alert B-52s used as missile carriers would suffice, or 77 B-1-type missile carriers. Used as penetrating bombers, 257 alert B-52s would be needed or 216 alert B-1s. Second, the missile carrier forces would be less sensitive in that they would not depend on decoy deception for penetration. Third, the defenses assumed in these calculations are, of course, not necessarily the same. In the absence of effective ECM, the force required to inflict the damage indicated on the B-52s might be totally incapable against the B-1s and ALCMs; similarly, a defense capable of dealing with B-1s and B-52s might not be able to even see the ALCMs.

Effects of High-Performance Terminal Defenses

In addition to advanced area defenses, the Soviet Union could conceivably deploy SAMs with very good low-altitude capabilities. If these were of sufficiently high quality, they could attack long-range subsonic cruise missiles. It seems highly unlikely that SAMs capable of shooting down SRAMs can be deployed, however, because of the SRAM's small radar cross section, its high supersonic speed, and its low-altitude capabilities. The penetrating bombers loaded with SRAMs would therefore be insensitive to these terminal defenses.

Even to attack subsonic cruise missiles, the SAMs would have to have high kill probabilities at altitudes of about 100 feet. The deployment of

Table 5-2. Modified B-52s or B-1s Required to Deliver 1,200 SRAMs to Targets
against Area Defenses of Different Effectiveness[a]

Number of kills area defense can enforce	Alert surviving bombers required to deliver 1,200 SRAMs	Decoys per bomber	Delivery of 1-megaton equivalents offense can enforce
0	62	0.0	400
200	117	6.1	166
400	147	8.1	240
600	172	9.3	292
800	195	10.2	340
1,000	216	10.9	379

a. Assuming 24 SRAM and decoy spaces per B-1 or modified B-52, no prelaunch attrition, and bomber and missile reliabilities of 90 percent each. SRAMs and decoys each carry 200-kiloton warheads. No account is taken of bombs carried by modified B-52s and B-1s or of other bomber aircraft. The mathematical model on which this table is based appears in appendix C. For each threat level, we selected a number of decoys per bomber that minimizes the number of bombers needed to deliver 1,200 reliable SRAMs. In the model we assumed that the defense could enforce the number of kills shown in the first column, regardless of the number of penetrators (bombers plus decoys), providing only that the number of penetrators entering the air defenses would exceed the number of kills.

such SAMs would mean that additional capabilities would have to be added to the cruise missile force if U.S. policy required the bomber force to be capable of attacking such terminally defended targets without ICBM or SLBM support. The discussion that follows is intended to develop an approximate characterization of the nature and scale of these additional capabilities.

Terminal defenses that might be able to attack long-range cruise missiles successfully fall into two broad classes: (1) SAMs that would have relatively limited range capabilities, and (2) longer-range terminal de-

Table 5-3. Missile Carriers Required to Deliver 1,200 ALCMs against
Area Defenses of Different Effectiveness[a]

Number of kills area defense can enforce	Type of alert surviving missile carriers required to deliver 1,200 ALCMs[b]			Delivery of 1-megaton equivalents offense can enforce
	18-missile	35-missile	50-missile	
0	82	42	30	400
200	96	49	35	400
400	110	56	40	400
600	123	63	44	400
800	137	71	49	400
1,000	151	77	54	400

a. The mathematical model on which this table is based appears in appendix C. Enough reliable missile carriers are provided at each threat level to ensure that the number of kills indicated in the first column could be accepted by the force while delivering 1,200 reliable ALCMs.

b. Eighteen missiles per missile carrier corresponds to a B-52, 35 to a fast hard missile carrier modeled on the lines of the B-1, and 50 to a missile carrier modeled on the lines of the Boeing 747 or C-5. It is assumed that cruise missiles carry 200-kiloton warheads, there is no prelaunch attrition, and missile carrier and missile reliabilities are 90 percent each.

fenses utilizing the same technologies as the area defenses outlined previously; that is, airborne radars and long-range manned or unmanned interceptors.

SAMs that can function at an altitude as low as 100 feet would probably be quite range-limited simply because a target at this low altitude cannot be seen very far away. For example, on a spherical earth with a flat terrain, an object 100 feet high is below the horizon to an observer at the earth's surface if the object is about ten miles away. If the observer is elevated to 200 feet, say, he can see the object farther away—about twenty-five miles in this case.

For SAM radars to function at such low altitudes, they also would need to be able to detect targets cloaked by reflections from the ground. Therefore SAM radars would require extremely narrow beams and hence relatively large antennas since the beam width is related inversely to antenna dimensions. A SAM radar designed to deal with missiles that could attack in relatively large numbers would also be likely to be a phased array radar to give it the ability to handle several engagements at one time. In practice, where terrain is not generally smooth, engagements are likely to start at relatively short ranges because of visibility problems. Thus the SAM site must have short reaction times, perhaps ten seconds or so. For all of these reasons, SAMs of this kind are apt to be much like the U.S. SAM-D and thus quite expensive.[20]

In order to illustrate how defenses of this kind would affect standoff bomber forces, we will consider the deployment of 200, 400, 600, and 800 such SAM sites around the fifty largest Soviet cities. We will assume that the terrain is smooth, thus eliminating the possibility of cruise missiles exploiting terrain and man-made features to escape SAMs.[21] We will

20. Estimates made at the Brookings Institution in 1972 put SAM-D unit investment costs at $20 million per firing unit. Four hundred such units, for example, could cost as much as $8 billion (fiscal 1972 dollars). Thus a combined high-performance area and terminal defense of the sort discussed in this paper could easily come to $20 billion in investment costs.

21. The assumptions made about these terminal defenses are conservative from the point of view of the offensive planner. In most practical cases it would probably be difficult to obtain complete SAM coverage around a large city at an altitude of about 100 feet because of roughness in the terrain. Moreover, cruise missiles attacking in substantial numbers over a short period at this low altitude would be difficult targets. A range of tactics would be available to these missiles—maneuvering in the terminal areas and "salvage" fuzing, to name two (salvage fuzing would result in the warhead of the cruise missile exploding at full yield if the cruise missile were successfully attacked by Soviet air defenses). These and other considerations seriously complicate the deployment of terminal defenses effective against cruise missiles.

Table 5-4. Number of SAM Sites That Would Have to Be Destroyed to Give Cruise Missiles Unimpeded Access to the 50 Largest Soviet Cities[a]

Number of SAM sites defending 50 largest cities	SAM site lethal radius (nautical miles)			
	5	7	9	15
	Number of SAM sites to be destroyed			
200	42	58	71	91
400	83	116	142	182
600	125	174	213	273
800	167	232	284	364
	Percentage of SAM sites to be destroyed			
	21	29	36	46

a. Assuming SAMs would be deployed on a circle with a radius equal to 1.5 times the radius of a circle that encloses 95 percent of the built-up parts of the city, and that SAM fields of fire are limited so that no more than 50 percent of the SAMs at a city can be used to defend along a single axis of attack. The mathematical model on which this table is based appears in appendix C.

further assume that these sites are deployed in defense perimeters at the outskirts of the cities in such a way that the linear *density* of SAM defenses is in proportion to the population of the cities. Thus an attacker attempting to cut a channel through these defenses would find each target equally attractive or unattractive.

Table 5-4 shows how many sites would have to be destroyed to cut channels to all fifty cities wide enough for cruise missiles to fly through unimpeded. The independent variables are the size of the SAM deployment and the radius over which a SAM could successfully attack cruise missiles.

To estimate the effects of such terminal defenses on cruise missile carrier forces, we use nine nautical miles as the representative limit on the lethal radius of SAM sites, in effect assuming that the SAM sites could initiate attacks on the cruise missiles as they come over the radar horizon for radars at ground level. The number of missile carriers that would have to be added to the alert missile forces shown in tables 5-1 through 5-3 to provide enough ALBMs to target two alert ALBM reentry vehicles to each SAM site in order to destroy the sites are shown below:[22]

22. Alert missile carriers are calculated to be able to carry the required number of ALBMs. Such targeting would result in a 96–99 percent probability of each site being destroyed by ALBMs with respective reliabilities of 80 and 90 percent. With respect to heavily defended targets, the lower of these two values would leave a significant probability that at least one site might survive. This could provide some incentive to target a third reentry vehicle, which would of course increase the force levels shown.

Number of SAM sites defending 50 largest cities	Alert surviving ALBMs required	Additional alert surviving missile carriers required		
		18 ALCMs or 1 ALBM	35 ALCMs or 2 ALBMs	50 ALCMs or 3 ALBMs
200	14	14	7	5
400	28	28	14	10
600	43	43	22	14
800	57	57	29	19

Should the Soviet Union choose mobile components, such as airborne radars and mobile or airborne missile launchers, instead of SAMs for terminal defense, the ALBMs would be directed away from the defenses to the targets themselves, since suppression attacks to help the cruise missiles penetrate would be much more difficult. Direct attacks on the cities themselves rather than on their defenses would require the delivery of perhaps 500–600 50-kiloton reentry vehicles. Each of these direct attacks would apply overpressure of at least 5 pounds per square inch to the entire area of the fifty largest cities.[23]

An attack of this kind would require a total of about sixty-eight alert ALBMs carried on thirty-four alert missile carriers (two ALBMs on each) or on twenty-three alert missile carriers (three ALBMs on each). The requirement for alert missile carriers with cruise missiles (which would attack undefended targets) would of course be reduced by the direct application of ALBMs to the fifty largest cities. The reduction would amount to approximately the following:

Alert missile carriers	Number of cruise missiles per missile carrier
15	18
8	35
5	50

The following net additions to the alert missile carriers represent the rough upper limits on the effects that terminal defenses could have on a standoff force:

23. Based on data from Geoffrey Kemp, "Nuclear Forces for Medium Powers, Parts II and III: Strategic Requirements and Options," *Adelphi Papers,* no. 107 (London: International Institute for Strategic Studies, Autumn 1974), pp. 23–26.

Alert missile carriers	*Number of cruise missiles per missile carrier*
53	18
26	35
18	50

Mobile terminal defenses would also complicate the task of the penetrating bomber. At a minimum they would force the penetrating bombers to stand off farther. SRAMs in a semiballistic mode might have sufficient range to overfly such defenses, but it is conceivable that a longer-range missile might be needed by the penetrating bomber as well. Thus the penetrating bombers could be forced into standoff attacks on terminally defended targets, with the only difference between penetrating and standoff systems being the range of the standoff missile used.

Effects of Area Defenses Using Mobile High-Performance SAMs

SAMs might also be used as area defenses. For example, the portion of the Soviet Union west of the Urals contains most of the large cities and hence most of the people and industry. This region covers about 1 million square nautical miles and lies within a circle about 600 nautical miles in radius. Mobile SAMs might be deployed randomly in this area or in a belt around its perimeter of roughly 3,800 nautical miles. If the SAMs were moved often enough to prevent the United States from detecting most of their locations, they would not be vulnerable to preplanned suppression attacks, and penetrating bombers and missiles would have to cope with the SAMs as they were encountered.

While theoretical calculations suggest that SAMs deployed in the Soviet Union in this manner could be highly effective, a host of practical problems makes their actual effectiveness highly problematical. For one thing, these SAMs would need a substantial degree of mobility—the radars, missiles, and fire control centers, for example, might have to be mounted on tracked vehicles to give a degree of cross-country mobility. The SAMs would also need to be competent to shoot down penetrators such as cruise missiles, B-1s, and B-52s. Their deployment would be constrained by terrain, forests, limited road networks, weather, and other natural and man-made features. Furthermore, they would be vulnerable to up-to-date intelligence, since the pinpointing of a significant number of SAMs along a single penetration route would compromise the whole system—the SAMs could be destroyed, and the bomber or cruise missile force could pour through the resulting channel.

Penetrating aircraft or missiles might also be able to detect radiations from SAM batteries before the SAMs could initiate an attack on the penetrators. In this event the SAMs could simply be avoided. In an operation of this sort, a manned aircraft, such as the B-52 or B-1, would have an advantage over cruise missiles. On the other hand, the smaller and more numerous cruise missiles would be more difficult targets. In addition, large numbers of cruise missiles, relatively closely spaced and penetrating along a single axis, might simply overwhelm the SAMs in the penetration corridor. Finally, the entire mobile SAM defense could be overflown by ballistic missiles.

Mid-Course Threats

The possibility has been suggested that standoff missile carriers, if deployed in relatively small numbers, say fifty, could be attacked by air defense fighters that would fly far out to meet the incoming carriers before they could launch their missiles.[24] It seems obvious that a penetrating force with larger numbers of aircraft, say 150, could be attacked as well by fighters at such long ranges.

The primary problem that would have to be solved to develop such a defensive system would be how to acquire information at very long ranges on the location and speeds of incoming bombers or missile carriers.[25] Putting enough fighters out to attack 50 or even 150 aircraft would be a less difficult task, though very long-range fighters would be needed. Such a threat would require both forces to take offsetting actions, which might include the following:

—*Moving critical mission events farther away from Soviet borders.* For the missile carrier this implies launching missiles from farther away. This possibility could be anticipated in the missile design by giving the cruise missiles excess range, especially at high altitude where these missiles can be very efficient. For the penetrating bomber, this means moving the refueling point back farther. Both the B-1 and B-52 probably have

24. "The Department of Defense Program of Research, Development, Test and Evaluation, FY 1976," p. V-17.

25. Evidently the Defense Department had difficulty defining the command and control system for such a defense and consequently did not evaluate the effects of this kind of defense in the Joint Strategic Bomber Study. See letter, Senator Thomas J. McIntyre to Secretary of Defense James R. Schlesinger, March 14, 1975.

enough range to allow for this eventuality, though some of the deeper targets might then be out of reach and would have to be attacked with missiles. It is not clear whether the penetrating or the standoff aircraft would have the advantage if launch and refuelling points were moved farther from Soviet territory.

—*Multiplying the directions of attack.* By threatening attacks from many directions, U.S. forces could make it necessary for the Soviet Union to multiply its defensive requirements several times, since all or part of the attack could come from any of the directions that had been demonstrated to be feasible. Either bombers or missile carriers could do this effectively.

—*Defending offensive aircraft.* Because air defense fighters would fly at high altitude and would have high-powered radars, the bombers or missile carriers would have good chances to defend themselves with long-range nuclear-armed bomber defense missiles. Either missile carriers or bombers could employ them, but efficient larger aircraft, such as missile carriers, could probably better afford to give up the payload to this purpose than the penetrating bomber.

—*Initiating low-altitude flight farther out.* Missile carriers and bombers could go to relatively low altitude to force the long-range fighters into a lookdown, shootdown mode. Missile carriers would probably suffer less than bombers from engaging in these tactics because of their payload and fuel capacity and because of their simpler missions.

Other tactics might also be considered, including the use of decoys, the use of tankers as decoys, and the suppression of air defense command and control systems with ballistic missiles. In any event, either bombers or missile carriers have a wide range of tactical possibilities to deal with such air defense fighters, but it is difficult to judge which would be more adaptable to such a development.

Arms Control Considerations

The potential effect of the ABM treaty on bomber penetration of high-performance air defenses has already been discussed at some length. We believe, therefore, that keeping this treaty in force is an important arms control measure supporting the future viability of the bomber force.

Limits on air defenses, while superficially appealing, are probably impractical because air defenses for general purpose forces are not distinguishable from strategic air defenses. Thus it seems unlikely that either side would agree to qualitative or quantitative limits on SAMs, intercep-tors, or air defense control systems such as AWACS. The large asymmetry that now exists between U.S. and Soviet air defenses would further com-plicate the negotiation of limits on air defenses.

There are arms control measures that could hurt the bomber forces, especially measures pertaining to bomber armament. The 600-kilometer limit on ALBMs in the Vladivostok agreement is a case in point. Similar limits on ALCMs would be much more serious because they would vir-tually prohibit the use of these missiles in large numbers.[26] Limitations that would deny the bomber force both ALCMs and long-range decoys (which would be practically indistinguishable from ALCMs) would seri-ously reduce the effectiveness of all the bomber types discussed in this chapter.

The question of whether an arms control agreement should ban or limit cruise missiles having more than a specified range is an important one, with implications that go beyond the scope of this study. We address the ques-tion only from the standpoint of the effectiveness and economics of the strategic bomber force. We point out that any limitation that would pre-vent the deployment of cruise missiles with sufficient range to hit Soviet targets from standoff bombers would severely inhibit all of the major op-tions we discuss. Moreover, weapons of this type are effective in a retalia-tory role but relatively ineffective in preemptive use. They add signifi-cantly to the deterrent capability of the bomber force and have marked economic advantages over the other systems that are examined in this study. This does not settle the question of whether such a ban should be imposed, but bomber force effectiveness is one aspect of the question that needs to be taken into account.

Summary

Air defenses capable of the performance attributed to the hypothetical defenses outlined in this chapter are not now available to the Soviet Union. The strongest air defenses in history—those in North Vietnam and in the

26. In answer to a question during a briefing on December 3, 1974, William Beecher, acting assistant secretary of defense for public affairs, said in substance that the Vladivostok limit on air-launched missiles applies to ballistic missiles, not to cruise missiles. It is now apparent, however, that the Soviet Union does not agree with this interpretation; thus what limits, if any, are to be imposed on such missiles has become a major issue in the strategic arms negotiations.

Sinai during the Arab-Israeli war in October 1973—were unable to inflict attrition levels that would be of any significance in strategic warfare. These air defenses were the result of more than two decades of development. Thus to develop defenses in the next five to ten years of the sort hypothesized would require sharply discontinuous developments—technological breakthroughs, if you will. Though breakthroughs cannot be ruled out, a more likely course is one of continuing gradual improvement, which means that such air defenses are far in the future—at least ten years or more. Even if strong strategic air defenses do appear, they almost certainly will remain ineffective against, and vulnerable to, ballistic missile attack. The United States therefore will retain the option to provide the mutual support of SLBMs and ICBMs to its bombers, and to the extent that U.S. strategists are willing to employ ballistic missiles in the bomber force, air defenses can simply be overflown.

Even if the United States rejects mutual support and insists that its bomber force must attack *through* air defenses, either standoff or penetrating forces can adapt to a wide range of air defense developments. Under certain circumstances the standoff force would have to rely on ALBMs for at least part of the deterrent task, but the penetrating force could also be forced into standoff ballistic or semiballistic attacks. All in all, penetrating bombers do not appear to have particular advantages over standoff weapon systems in penetrating air defenses.

CHAPTER SIX

ANALYSIS OF ALTERNATIVE FORCES

The analyses presented thus far show that there is more than one way to fulfill U.S. needs for a strategic bomber force. For example, a number of variables over which the United States has control affect both the survivability and the penetration capabilities of the strategic bomber force and can be traded off among each other. How the threats to bombers will evolve is of course uncertain. To integrate these and other considerations, we compare five alternative bomber forces that embody different trade-offs, reflect different judgments about the role of bombers, and have essentially equal effectiveness when faced with severe threats. Assuming that the forces stabilize at the 1985 levels, we estimate the performance of each against four postulated threats. The most severe of these threats probably would not evolve until well past 1985.

The Military Task

The retaliatory task used as the standard for all the forces is the delivery of the equivalent of 400 megatons of nuclear weapons on the Soviet urban industrial target system. As we explained in chapter 2, this requirement can be translated into approximately 1,200 weapons of the size carried by present and planned U.S. attack missiles. In setting this task we assumed that the bomber force would have the advantage of strategic warning, most likely during a crisis situation, and would operate at the highest possible alert rate, but we also evaluate the operation of the forces on a routine day-to-day basis.

Threat Variations

We arranged the threats in four levels of decreasing ability to destroy the bombers and their missiles either on the ground before launch or in the air during the penetration phase. The most severe threat (Level 1) postulates a Soviet capability to launch 300 submarine-launched ballistic missiles (SLBMs) against U.S. bomber bases, on depressed trajectories with a flight time of about 420 seconds. We further assumed a Soviet area air defense deployment that could exact 400 intercepts on the penetrating bomber and cruise missile force, and a high-performance terminal air defense force of 400 surface-to-air missile (SAM) sites located at the fifty largest cities in the Soviet Union. These defensive SAMs are postulated to have the capability to effectively intercept the air-launched cruise missile (ALCM). This postulation necessitates the suppression of the SAMs for cruise missile penetration by supersonic missiles, such as short-range attack missiles (SRAMs), or an air-launched ballistic missile (ALBM).

For Level 2 we relaxed the SLBM threat to bomber prelaunch survivability by changing from depressed trajectories to a minimum-energy trajectory. The flight time of the SLBMs attacking the bomber bases is thereby increased from 420 seconds to 900 seconds. Area air defenses and terminal defenses are the same as in Level 1.

For Level 3 we assumed the effectiveness of the terminal air defenses to be comparable to present-day Soviet SAM systems. Since the low-altitude intercept capability of these systems is small, it would be unnecessary to suppress them in order for low-flying bombers and cruise missiles to penetrate to the targets. The capable area air defenses of lookdown, shootdown fighters controlled by aircraft such as airborne warning and control systems (AWACS), however, remain in Level 3.

Finally, Level 4 represents the capability of current Soviet air defenses, which are virtually ineffective against U.S. penetrating bombers, SRAMs, and cruise missiles. The SLBM threat to prelaunch survivability is considered negligible since few Soviet ballistic missile submarines are positioned close enough to threaten U.S. bomber bases.

The four threat levels are summarized below:

Threat level	Prelaunch threat	Area air defenses	Terminal air defenses
1	300 depressed trajectory SLBMs	400 effective intercepts	400 low-altitude SAM sites at 50 cities
2	300 minimum-energy trajectory SLBMs	400 effective intercepts	400 low-altitude SAM sites at 50 cities
3	300 minimum-energy trajectory SLBMs	400 effective intercepts	Negligible
4	Negligible	Negligible	Negligible

Characteristics of the Alternative Forces

We were guided by the following considerations in the design of the forces required to cope with the four threat levels:

—Any alternative must use the existing force as a departure point. There are lengthy lead times involved in developing and procuring new weapons. Thus we programmed the five forces through ten years (1976–85) to fully realize each alternative posture.

—We limited the alternatives to the extent that the forces utilized only technologies that are under development or active investigation. During the next ten years, it is possible but unlikely that changes will occur in concepts, policies, or technology that will greatly alter the relationships between offensive and defensive forces.

With these factors in mind, we derived the different force types that could be attained by 1985 to accomplish the specified retaliatory task with strategic warning against the most severe threat, Level 1. These forces are shown in table 6-1.

Force 1 consists of 255 modified B-52s and a like number of supporting tankers. According to former Secretary of the Air Force John L. McLucas, B-52s could have new engines, a new supercritical wing, an extended bomb bay that could carry up to twenty-four SRAMs, improved avionics, and low-level ride control.[1] In addition, we have assumed that the improved B-52s would be equipped with rockets to speed their takeoff.

Force 2 includes 200 B-1s and thus is similar to Air Force planning, which provides for 210 B-1s. An advanced tanker would gradually replace the older KC-135 starting in 1981.

Forces 3, 4, and 5 all carry air-launched cruise missiles as their primary armament. Force 3 would utilize a wide-bodied transport as the missile carrier and would require an advanced tanker to support the airborne alert. Force 4 would be a new, smaller "fast hard" aircraft like the B-1 but without a supersonic high-altitude capability. In Force 5 the wide-bodied transport aircraft would be accelerated by rocket assist. Neither Force 4 nor 5 needs tanker support.

We assumed that these forces would operate routinely at a ground alert rate of 60 percent. In time of crisis a noteworthy change in the operational

1. "B-1 Development Program," Statement of Honorable John L. McLucas, Secretary of the Air Force, Presentation to the Senate Armed Services Committee, Research and Development Subcommittee (April 17, 1975; processed).

Table 6-1. Alternative Forces Designed for Approximately Equal Effectiveness against Threat Level 1

Force	Number and type of aircraft[a]	Number and type of tankers	Number of dispersal bases	Number of air-to-surface missiles
1	255 improved B-52s	255 KC-135s and advanced tankers	100	6,120 SRAMs and armed decoys
2	200 B-1s	200 KC-135s and advanced tankers	75	4,800 SRAMs and armed decoys
3	80 cruise missile carriers	80 advanced tankers	(airborne alert)	3,100 ALCMs 54 ALBMs
4	105 fast hard cruise missile carriers	None	75	2,660 ALCMs 58 ALBMs
5	120 high-acceleration cruise missile carriers	None	100	3,185 ALCMs 58 ALBMs

a. We assume that all soft aircraft can resist 1 psi overpressure and hard aircraft, 3 psi. The flyout characteristics are shown in figure 4-1. Soft missile carriers in Force 3 are assumed to carry fifty cruise missiles or three ALBMs; in forces 4 and 5, thrity-five cruise missiles or two ALBMs. The modified B-52s and B-1s are both assumed to have twenty-four spaces each for SRAMs, and decoys are assumed to displace one SRAM each.

mode of Force 3 would occur in that 60 percent of the force would go on airborne alert to nullify any possible threats to its prelaunch survivability. Forces 1, 2, 4, and 5 would go to an 85 percent alert level. These forces are assumed to receive tactical warning within ninety seconds of the launch of enemy SLBMs and to successfully initiate takeoff within another sixty seconds to escape the lethal effects of a surprise attack. When forces are on a day-to-day alert basis, a bomber reaction time of 270 seconds is used rather than the 150 seconds for a crisis alert status. In order to dilute the enemy attack and to avoid queuing delays, the ground alert forces are assumed to be dispersed over the number of interior bases shown in table 6-1.

In Force 1 the number of decoys was chosen to maximize the number of SRAMs delivered and in Force 2, to minimize the number of bombers needed. Higher penetration probabilities could be achieved with larger numbers of decoys, but this would increase the required number of bombers and thus the cost of Force 2.

Analytical Results

The estimated performance of the five alternative bomber forces against the most demanding threat (Level 1) is shown in table 6-2. An important

Table 6-2. Estimated Performance of the Five Alternative Bomber Forces against Threat Level 1

Force	Strategic warning				Day-to-day alert
	Prelaunch survivability for alert force (percent)	*Number of aircraft surviving SLBM attack*	*Penetration probability (percent)*	*Attack missile delivery capability*	*Prelaunch survivability for alert force (percent)*
1	74	160	66	1,371	22
2	87	148	63	1,220	31
3	100[a]	48	76	1,270	...[b]
4	87	74	75	1,190	31
5	74	75	75	1,220	22

a. For the airborne alert force only.
b. Negligible.

result of these estimates is that the bomber force could not be expected to survive such a severe prelaunch threat when operated on a routine day-to-day basis. None of the forces under consideration here have an adequate number of survivors when attacked by depressed trajectory missiles as postulated in threat Level 1 while on a day-to-day alert status. To survive a surprise attack, a force would have to be much harder, have a much shorter reaction time, or be much larger than any considered here. We believe, however, that incorporating such features in the bomber force would be only marginally practical at best.

Since all the forces were designed to be roughly equal in performance against the most severe threat, given strategic warning, the measure of comparison for these equally effective forces would be their relative costs, which are shown in table 6-3 in billions of fiscal year 1976 dollars. Two sets of costs are involved: ten-year costs, separated into investment and operating costs; and the annual operating cost at which the forces would stabilize after having reached their design goals in about 1985.

The relative differences in these projected costs are significant. Force 1, consisting of modified B-52s, has slightly lower investment costs than the B-1 force. The operating costs are higher, however, because of the larger number of aircraft and the force structure. The B-1 force is relatively more expensive than the cruise missile forces because of the larger number of aircraft that must be purchased, incurring both high procurement and operating costs.

The choice between Forces 3, 4, and 5 should not be made exclusively

Table 6-3. Estimated Ten-Year Costs of the Five Alternative Bomber Forces and Annual Operating Costs in 1985

Costs in billions of fiscal 1976 dollars

Force	Number and type of aircraft	Ten-year costs			Annual operating costs, fiscal 1985
		Invest-ment	Oper-ating	Total	
1	255 B-52s	34.2	35.4	69.6	3.8
2	200 B-1s	37.2	34.2	71.3	3.3
3	80 cruise missile carriers	27.3	27.8	55.1	1.7
4	100 fast hard cruise missile carriers	29.0	30.6	59.6	2.1
5	120 high-acceleration cruise missile carriers	29.7	31.0	60.7	2.3

on the basis of cost, since the differences between them are not that great. Rather, the choice should be made on the basis of the difference in the basing modes in time of crisis. Those who have more confidence in the current ground alert system that depends on strategic *and* tactical warning would prefer either Force 4 or 5. Those who have more confidence in the survivability of an airborne alert force, which depends only on strategic warning, would choose Force 3. The latter force would cost the least, both during the transition period through 1985 and beyond. After 1985 the operating cost of the standoff forces would be substantially less than for the penetrating forces.

An analysis of the performance of the alternative forces against lesser threats supplies other useful information. In table 6-4 the number of attack missiles each force would be capable of delivering against threats at levels 2, 3, and 4 is compared.

With strategic warning each of the forces would have a capability in excess of that required for the retaliatory task. This suggests that the B-52 force can be modernized and dispersed in order to be effective well into the 1980s if the United States is willing to rely on strategic warning and on ground alert.

From a day-to-day alert posture, Forces 2, 3, and 4 would fall short of the standard of 1,200 missiles delivered against a Level 2 threat. Against a Level 3 threat, the standoff forces would be marginally better than the manned penetrators. Against the estimated current threat (Level 4), all would possess a more than adequate capability to deal with the retaliatory mission.

Table 6-4. Comparison of the Capability of the Five Alternative Bomber Forces to Deliver Attack Missiles against Threat Levels 2, 3, and 4

Force	Number and type of aircraft	Threat level 2	Threat level 3[a]	Threat level 4[a]
			Attack missile delivery capability	
	With strategic warning			
1	255 improved B-52s	2,010	2,020	3,960
2	200 B-1s	1,500	1,500	3,110
3	80 cruise missile carriers	1,700[b]	2,150[b]	2,590[b]
4	100 fast hard cruise missile carriers	1,500	1,990	2,270
5	120 high-acceleration cruise missile carriers	1,900	2,380	2,720
	Day-to-day alert			
1	255 improved B-52s	1,180	1,180	2,800
2	200 B-1s	850	850	2,200
3	80 cruise missile carriers	450	1,340	1,830
4	100 fast hard cruise missile carriers	760	1,270	1,600
5	120 high-acceleration cruise missile carriers	1,020	1,530	1,920

a. Adjusted to maximize attack missiles delivered.
b. For these threat levels, this force utilizes ground alert.

Possible Evolution of Threats and Forces

Another way to think about these forces is to consider how they would evolve as the threat might grow from the current estimate (Level 4) to the most severe postulation (Level 1). Forces 2 and 4 anticipate the development of a depressed trajectory threat by requiring that the United States pay for the hardness and speed needed to resist such a threat before it occurs. Forces 3 and 5, on the other hand, could be managed so as not to require such anticipation. If the B-52s, equipped with standoff missiles, can be adapted for airborne alert or if they can be alternatively equipped with a rocket-assisted takeoff capability, versions of Forces 3 and 5, employing B-52s as missile carriers, might be similarly managed. In effect, if strategists opted for Force 3, they might decide not to buy tankers to support airborne alert until serious threats to prelaunch survivability seemed more probable. Since the tankers would be modified aircraft such as Boeing 747s, and since production lines for aircraft of this class are likely to be open for many years, tanker procurement could be made relatively quickly if the need arose. Similarly, for Force 5, devices to quickly accelerate the cruise missile carrier need not be procured until a threat to prelaunch survivability becomes more apparent.

Forces 3, 4, and 5 could be equipped with ballistic missiles only when a terminal defense threat to cruise missiles appeared imminent. Forces 3 and 5 would probably be more flexible in this regard, since they might rely essentially on civilian-type aircraft that would remain in production for a long time. Thus the procurement of even the aircraft needed to carry the ALBMs might be deferred.

By including SRAMs in Forces 1 and 2, these forces would be adapted, before the need arises, to the deployment of terminal defenses.

None of the forces must be preadapted for area defense developments; Forces 3 and 5, because of their possible use of civilian-type aircraft, would be the most flexible. Buying aircraft before they are needed in Forces 2 and 4 might be necessary, but armed decoys for Forces 1 and 2 could be delayed until area defenses seemed likely. Such delays in developing a B-1 decoy are current Air Force policy.

On balance, Forces 3 and 5 seem best suited to sequential adaptations to increasing threats.

It might be argued that the way the USSR decides to develop its defensive forces will depend on the type of bomber force the United States selects. This argument would apply, of course, to any of the five alternative bomber forces. It would seem that Forces 1 and 2 are most vulnerable to such Soviet action since the number of penetrating bombers needed increases rapidly as the deployment of high-performance area defenses increases. (AWACS and lookdown, shootdown fighters have already been developed by the United States for general purpose forces.) While the standoff forces (3, 4, and 5) might have to respond to terminal defense deployments, the technology available to them in the form of ALBMs and the fact that many deployed SAMs can be avoided reduce the size of the needed response to terminal defense deployments. Forces 1 and 2, equipped with SRAMs from the outset, are insensitive to the development of such defenses. Forces 3 and 5, unlike Forces 2 and 4, have the added advantage of being less likely to require anticipatory purchases of aircraft.

CHAPTER SEVEN

CONCLUSIONS AND RECOMMENDATIONS

This analysis, like others of such complex issues, leaves room for differing judgments about the policies that should govern the design of the bomber force, about the evolution of future threats, and about the role of the bomber force. We have been limited by the necessity to rely on unclassified data, and our simple modeling techniques capture only the most important properties of the problems treated. Nevertheless we believe that the broad direction that decisions concerning the bomber force should take is quite clearly delineated by the conclusions of this analysis. In summary, these conclusions are as follows:

—The effectiveness of the current bomber force is more than adequate now and, with minor force modifications, will remain so in the future under foreseeable conditions. With the planned deployment of ten Trident submarines, U.S. strategic forces will rise approximately to the limits established in the Vladivostok guidelines.[1] Thus there is no urgency to make major changes now, although modernization will be necessary eventually.

—There are marked economic advantages for a bomber force that carries standoff missiles, which would be an alternative to the B-1 in modernizing the bomber force.

—There appear to be no significant military advantages to be gained by deploying a new penetrating bomber such as the B-1 in preference to this alternative.

—In light of these findings, we see no reason to make a commitment to produce the B-1, and we believe there is considerable justification for exploring alternatives based on the use of standoff missiles.

Our more detailed conclusions follow and touch on each of the points we have considered in this report.

1. Joint Soviet-American Statement on Strategic Arms Limitation, November 24, 1974.

Need for a Bomber Force

We consider the sea-based missile force to be the cornerstone of the future U.S. strategic capability and to be particularly well-suited to the retaliatory mission because of the relative invulnerability of sea-based missiles to a surprise or preemptive attack. While the number of land-based missiles possessed by the United States has political value in maintaining essential equivalence—now stressed in U.S. strategic policy—these missiles, if actually faced with Soviet deployment of accurate multiple independently targetable reentry vehicles, would assume a secondary retaliatory role and would contribute mainly to a strategic warfighting capability. If their military worth were to be diminished for this reason, the United States should shift its reliance on land-based missiles to sea-based missiles. The Trident program, which has already been started, provides a suitable basis for this shift.

We believe that the proper military role of the bomber force in the future is to act as insurance against the failure of the ballistic missile forces. The amount this nation is willing to pay for such insurance and the amount of coverage that is desired depends on subjective judgments of the risks involved. The political purpose of the bombers is to help maintain essential equivalence with the USSR. The number of bombers in the force required for this purpose will depend partly on the value placed on them in any future accord that may be negotiated on the basis of the Vladivostok understanding.

Present Program

The B-1 program has reached a point in its development-procurement cycle that calls for a key decision—whether or not to make a commitment to produce the aircraft. If the commitment is made, spending on the B-1 will increase rapidly from about $750 million in fiscal year 1976 to about $2.5 billion annually in the late 1970s. There will be additional costs for short-range attack missiles to arm the B-1 and for a new tanker to refuel it. On the other hand, a decision not to proceed with the B-1 production program would not mean that the bomber force would rapidly become obsolete and ineffective, because the present aircraft will be structurally sound well into the 1990s, and there is only a remote possibility that any potential enemy action could threaten the military effectiveness of the B-52 force before that time. Furthermore, U.S. sea-based and land-based missile forces are effective hedges against an enemy threat directed specifically toward the bomber force within the same time frame.

Prelaunch Survivability

The value of the bomber force is greatest during a time of crisis because it can be placed on a higher alert status. We believe that either through assessment of a political crisis or through U.S. intelligence systems the United States will receive strategic warning adequate to increase the alert status of the bomber force. Secretary of Defense Schlesinger had expressed similar views in regard to strategic warning.[2]

The threat to bomber prelaunch survivability of a well-executed surprise attack is the most demanding problem for those charged with designing the bomber force. A surprise attack could be carried out by either depressed trajectory ballistic missiles or strategic cruise missiles launched from Soviet submarines. The likelihood of a surprise attack during a period of relative stability is extremely remote, however, and U.S. submarine-based ballistic missiles provide protection against such an unlikely contingency. Thus we believe that the United States does not need to rely on the bomber force to hedge against the possibility. In addition, the bomber force as currently planned, including the B-1, is not well-adapted to cope with such a threat. The current solution to the problem is to depend on a quick-reaction ground alert posture for the bomber force in order to flush the bombers upon receipt of tactical warning. Even with a bomber like the B-1, this reliance on ground alert and dispersal provides very narrow margins of safety if severe prelaunch threats materialize; these margins degrade rapidly with adverse changes in the performance of tactical warning systems or alert forces. High-acceleration devices such as rocket-assisted takeoff, reductions in bomber reaction time, and dispersal basing offer some promise of improving the prelaunch survivability of bombers on ground alert under conditions of strategic warning.

During the Cuban missile crisis the Air Force placed some of its bombers on airborne alert to assure their survivability and to demonstrate

2. "Report of Secretary of Defense James R. Schlesinger to the Congress on the FY 1976 and Transition Budgets, FY 1977 Authorization Request and FY 1976–1980 Defense Programs" (February 1975; processed), p. II-35.

resolve. We believe that this mode is virtually invulnerable to any threats that can now be anticipated, but reliance on airborne alert in time of crisis would put a premium on designing a bomber force with greater endurance than the one currently planned.

Penetration

The remaining threat to the retaliatory capability of the bomber force is the possible emergence of high-quality Soviet air defenses. A high-quality Soviet air defense system might include lookdown, shootdown interceptors guided by large airborne control centers and surface-to-air missiles with a low-altitude capability down to about 100 feet. Although this threat has been anticipated for some time, there is no evidence that it will materialize within the next several years. If such a system does not emerge, then the present force of B-52s has sufficient capability.[3] Moreover, our analysis suggests that if the B-52s were equipped with armed decoys or with long-range cruise missiles, exploiting fully their existing payload capabilities, they could cope with substantial deployments of advanced air defenses.

Recent testimony by Defense Department officials emphasizes the dependence of the currently planned bomber force of B-52s and B-1s on electronic countermeasures (ECM) to counter the threat of high-quality area air defenses.[4] We do not believe that ECM should be relied on to assure the penetration of the future bomber force. If government leaders conclude that ECM can guarantee the effectiveness of the penetrating bomber, however, then the sizing and evaluation of alternative forces should be based on this choice.

In our view, air-launched cruise missiles provide the most economical means of coping with sophisticated *area* defenses. The Defense Department is undertaking a deliberate program of developing these cruise missiles that appears to be properly paced to meet an area defense threat. These missiles can be carried on B-52s in the near term. The design of the follow-on carrier would now warrant initial study. If arms control agree-

3. The Defense Department has apparently come to a similar conclusion. See statement of Malcolm R. Currie, director of Defense Research and Engineering, *The Department of Defense Program of Research, Development, Test and Evaluation, FY 1976,* Hearings before the Senate Appropriations Committee, 94 Cong. 1 sess. (February 26, 1975), p. V-18.
4. Ibid., p. V-15.

ments should come into being that severely limit the deployment of air-launched cruise missiles with the required range, consideration could be given to the deployment of air-launched ballistic missiles for coping with area and terminal defenses.

We believe that U.S. strategic forces can adequately counter any deployment of fixed *terminal* surface-to-air missile (SAM) systems by suppressing them with sea-based or land-based ballistic missiles. Since the strategic missile forces are programmed to contain more than 7,000 reentry vehicles by the mid-1980s, the use of several hundred of them to destroy terminal SAMs would not significantly reduce their overall capability. We see little purpose in the further development of an air-launched ballistic missile (ALBM) for destroying SAMs in view of the capabilities of currently planned ballistic missile forces. But even if a choice is made to reject the use of intercontinental ballistic missiles or submarine-launched ballistic missiles (SLBMs) for air defense suppression, the development of an ALBM would not appear to be justified now by existing Soviet strategic SAMs.

Alternative Forces

A standoff bomber force is more economical than an equal-effectiveness B-1 force. As much as $10 billion to $15 billion might be saved in the first ten years after a decision to modernize by choosing the standoff force. Thus we believe that the production of the B-1 should not be approved and that the research and development program should be brought to a speedy conclusion as soon as the technological potential in the B-1 prototype program is fully exploited. Instead, systems studies and appropriate advanced development of a standoff bomber should begin. Emphasis should be given to those characteristics needed to assure adequate prelaunch survivability and low cost.

Arms Control Measures

In addition to these conclusions about the future development of the bomber force, we suggest that several pertinent strategic arms control measures should be pursued.

—The viability and effectiveness of the antiballistic missile treaty[5] should be preserved; this would protect the penetration capabilities of the ballistic missile forces. The potential for destruction of Soviet air defenses by ballistic missiles gives added assurance of bomber penetration.

—The United States should seek a ban on the testing and deployment of depressed trajectory SLBMs. Defense spokesmen have testified that a ban would be verifiable. By this means, a possible threat to bomber pre-launch survivability would be mitigated.

—The ultimate acceptability of an arms control agreement that bans or limits cruise missiles of more than a specified range—for example, 600 kilometers—rests on considerations that go beyond the scope of this study. Such limits, however, without radical controls on air defenses (and such controls seem unlikely), would severely limit all of the major options discussed in the study.

—Patrol limits on strategic ballistic missile submarines (SSBNs) should be considered. Such limits may now present serious verification problems, but ASW breakthroughs might change this. If ASW breakthroughs also reduced the survivability of SSBNs, the bomber force and consequently SSBN patrol limits would assume new importance.

5. Treaty between the United States of America and the Union of Soviet Socialist Republics on the Limitation of Anti-Ballistic Missile Systems, signed at Moscow, May 26, 1972.

Cost Methodology and Projections

The principal definitions and methods used in making cost estimates and projections in this staff study are similar to those used in other recent Brookings defense policy studies. The aggregated costs for the bomber force were developed from an examination of four types of expenditures: major-system acquisition costs, other investment costs, direct operating costs, and indirect operating costs.

Major-System Acquisition Costs

The acquisition costs of major systems include the costs of research, development, testing and engineering; procurement; and military construction for the major bomber program (aircraft, tankers, and air-to-surface missiles). Our sources for the estimates of acquisition costs were for the most part Department of Defense publications and Air Force testimony before the Senate Armed Services and Appropriations committees. Data were available from these sources for all the major systems except cruise missile carriers and air-launched ballistic missiles; we made our own estimates for these systems. In projecting the costs of the Air Force program shown in table 3-4 and the alternative force posture in table 6-3, no allowance was made for cost growth. Tables A-1 and A-2 show the estimated acquisition costs for the major systems.

Table A-1. Estimated Procurement Costs for the B-1 Bomber, 1976–83
Total obligational authority in millions of fiscal 1976 dollars

Item	1976	1977	1978	1979	1980	1981	1982	1983
Number procured	0	8	22	31	48	48	48	34
Cost of procurement	150	1,200	1,800	2,000	2,250	1,980	1,850	1,100

Source: *Fiscal Year 1975 Authorization for Military Procurement, Research and Development, and Active Duty, Selected Reserve and Civilian Personnel Strengths,* Hearings before the Senate Armed Services Committee, 93 Cong. 2 sess. (1974), pt. 7, p. 4000.

Table A-2. Estimated Costs of Various Bomber Force Components
Total obligational authority in millions of fiscal 1976 dollars

System	Total research, development, testing, and engineering costs	Average unit procurement cost[a]	Cost to reopen production line
About 100 advanced tankers	225	30	...
About 100 cruise missile carriers			
Wide-body transport type	500	60	...
Fast hard type	2,000	65	...
Short-range attack missile	...	0.5	100
Air-launched cruise missile and armed decoy	320	0.5	...
Air-launched ballistic missile	2,000	20	...

a. Excluding research, development, testing, and engineering.

The construction of each new dispersal base was estimated to cost $25 million. Based on Air Force testimony, the cost of modifying each B-52 (as shown in Force 1, chapter 6) was estimated to be $35 million in constant fiscal year 1976 dollars.

Other Investment Costs

Other investment costs include the remainder of research, development, testing, and engineering; procurement; and military construction costs that are required to support the manned bomber force. Examples of such costs are the procurement costs of test equipment, ground-support equipment, and systems used for communications or intelligence purposes. The costs of basic research for systems related to bombers and air-to-surface missiles would also fall in this category.

Other investment costs from the support program were allocated to the bomber force in proportion to major-system acquisition costs. This came to $1,260 million in fiscal 1976 dollars. Since we were unable to discern any consistent method to change other investment costs with other variables, such as force size or quality, these investment costs were held constant for all alternative postures.

Table A-3. **Annual Operating Costs of the Bomber Force on 40 Percent Alert and 60 Percent Alert**

Millions of fiscal 1976 dollars

Item	Operating costs	
	40 percent alert rate	*60 percent alert rate*
B-52 squadron	40	50
FB-111 squadron	26	33
KC-135 squadron	25	31
B-1 squadron	...	50
Cruise missile carrier	...	50
Advanced tanker squadron	...	33
Air-to-surface missile (per 1,000)	...	4
Air-launched ballistic missile (per missile)	...	1
Bomber dispersal base	...	5

Direct Operating Costs

Direct operating costs include the costs for military and civilian personnel and operation and maintenance costs attributable to the bomber force. These are clearly identifiable as operating costs for the strategic program package in various Department of Defense publications and in testimony before Congress. Thus direct operating costs can be calculated with a higher degree of confidence than other investment costs or indirect operating costs. The factors we derived are given in table A-3.

Indirect Operating Costs

Indirect operating costs are the military personnel and operations and maintenance costs included in the Defense Department's Program III (Intelligence and Communications), VI (Research and Development), VII (General Supply and Maintenance), VIII (Training, Medical, and Other Personnel Activities), and IX (Administration and Associated Activities) that are necessary to support the operations of the bomber force. In our analysis, we assumed that the indirect operating costs attributable to the bomber force were directly proportional to the direct operating costs. This assumption is heroic, but in the absence of better information on the precise relationship between support costs and mission forces, it appears to be as valid as any other.

Table A-4. Projected Systems and Costs, Force 1, Fiscal Years 1976–85

Total obligational authority in millions of fiscal 1976 dollars

Category	1976	1977	1978	1979	1980	1981	1982	1983	1984	1985	Average annual costs
Unit equipment											
B-52[a]	335	255	255	255	255	255	255	255	255	255	...
FB-111	66	0	0	0	0	0	0	0	0	0	...
Tanker	610	255	255	255	255	255	255	255	255	255	...
SRAM	1,140	1,140	1,140	1,640	2,140	2,640	3,140	3,640	4,080	4,080	...
ALCM	0	0	0	0	500	1,000	1,500	2,000	2,500	3,060	...
Costs											
Major system acquisition	310	445	810	2,390	3,390	3,910	3,910	3,890	1,290	1,290	2,164
Other investment	1,260	1,260	1,260	1,260	1,260	1,260	1,260	1,260	1,260	1,260	1,260
Direct operating	1,975	1,435	1,485	1,540	1,600	1,650	1,710	1,770	1,840	1,880	1,688
Indirect operating	2,015	1,690	1,720	1,750	1,790	1,820	1,860	1,890	1,930	1,960	1,843
Total	5,560	4,830	5,275	6,940	8,040	8,640	8,740	8,810	6,320	6,390	6,955

a. Bombers are dispersed on 100 interior bases.

Table A-5. Projected Systems and Costs, Force 2, Fiscal Years 1976–85

Total obligational authority in millions of fiscal 1976 dollars

Category	1976	1977	1978	1979	1980	1981	1982	1983	1984	1985	Average annual costs
Unit equipment											
B-52[a]	335	255	255	255	255	240	225	195	105	0	...
FB-111	66	0	0	0	0	0	0	0	0	0	...
B-1[a]	0	0	0	0	0	15	30	90	150	200	...
Tanker	610	255	255	255	255	255	255	255	255	200	...
SRAM	1,140	1,140	1,140	1,540	1,940	2,340	2,740	3,140	3,200	3,200	...
ALCM	0	0	0	0	400	800	1,200	1,600	1,600	1,600	...
Costs											
Major system acquisition	810	2,295	2,770	3,450	3,600	3,790	3,600	2,030	1,170	1,040	2,456
Other investment	1,260	1,260	1,260	1,260	1,260	1,260	1,260	1,260	1,260	1,260	1,260
Direct operating	1,975	1,385	1,435	1,490	1,545	1,595	1,660	1,715	1,775	1,560	1,614
Indirect operating	2,015	1,660	1,690	1,720	1,760	1,790	1,830	1,860	1,900	1,750	1,798
Total	6,060	6,600	7,155	7,920	8,165	8,435	8,350	6,865	6,105	5,610	7,128

a. Bombers are dispersed on 100 interior bases.

Table A-6. Projected Systems and Costs, Force 3, Fiscal Years 1976–85

Total obligational authority in millions of fiscal 1976 dollars

Category	1976	1977	1978	1979	1980	1981	1982	1983	1984	1985	Average annual costs
Unit equipment											
B-52[a]	335	255	255	255	255	210	165	120	75	0	...
FB-111	66	0	0	0	0	0	0	0	0	0	...
Missile carrier[a]	0	0	0	0	0	15	30	45	60	80	...
Tanker	610	255	255	255	255	225	185	165	135	80	...
SRAM	1,140	1,140	1,140	1,140	1,140	840	640	440	240	0	...
ALCM	0	0	0	0	0	600	1,200	1,800	2,400	3,100	...
ALBM	0	0	0	0	0	12	24	36	48	54	...
Costs											
Major system acquisition	60	695	1,670	2,840	2,190	2,190	2,190	2,750	140	0	1,473
Other investment	1,260	1,260	1,260	1,260	1,260	1,260	1,260	1,260	1,260	1,260	1,260
Direct operating	1,975	1,385	1,385	1,385	1,385	1,235	1,100	955	815	565	1,219
Indirect operating	2,015	1,660	1,660	1,660	1,660	1,570	1,490	1,400	1,320	1,170	1,561
Total	5,310	5,000	5,975	7,145	6,495	6,255	6,040	6,365	3,535	2,995	5,513

a. Bombers and missile carriers are based on thirty existing bases and are placed on airborne alert upon strategic warning.

Table A-7. Projected Systems and Costs, Force 4, Fiscal Years 1976–85

Total obligational authority in millions of fiscal 1976 dollars

Category	1976	1977	1978	1979	1980	1981	1982	1983	1984	1985	Average annual costs
Unit equipment											
B-52[a]	335	255	255	255	255	225	195	135	75	0	...
FB-111	66	0	0	0	0	0	0	0	0	0	...
Missile carrier[a]	0	0	0	0	0	15	30	60	90	100	...
Tanker	610	255	255	255	255	225	195	135	75	0	...
SRAM	1,140	1,140	1,140	1,140	1,140	840	640	440	240	0	...
ALCM	0	0	0	0	0	600	1,200	1,800	2,400	2,660	...
ALBM	0	0	0	0	0	12	24	36	48	48	...
Costs											
Major system acquisition	50	960	2,220	2,480	2,005	2,005	3,130	2,650	880	0	1,638
Other investment	1,260	1,260	1,260	1,260	1,260	1,260	1,260	1,260	1,260	1,260	1,260
Direct operating	1,975	1,385	1,435	1,485	1,535	1,485	1,430	1,285	1,115	785	1,392
Indirect operating	2,015	1,660	1,690	1,720	1,750	1,720	1,690	1,600	1,500	1,300	1,665
Total	5,300	5,265	6,605	6,945	6,550	6,470	7,510	6,795	4,755	3,345	5,954

a. Bombers and missile carriers are based on ninety interior bases.

Table A-8. Projected Systems and Costs, Force 5, Fiscal Years 1976–85

Total obligational authority in millions of fiscal 1976 dollars

Category	1976	1977	1978	1979	1980	1981	1982	1983	1984	1985	Average annual costs
Unit equipment											
B-52[a]	335	255	255	255	255	225	195	135	75	0	...
FB-111	66	0	0	0	0	0	0	0	0	0	...
Missile carrier[a]	0	0	0	0	0	15	30	60	90	120	...
Tanker	610	255	255	255	255	225	195	135	75	0	...
SRAM	1,140	1,140	1,140	1,140	1,140	840	640	440	240	0	...
ALCM	0	0	0	0	0	600	1,200	1,800	2,400	3,185	...
ALBM	0	0	0	0	0	12	24	36	48	58	...
Costs											
Major system acquisition	50	960	2,220	2,480	2,005	2,255	3,130	3,230	555	250	1,714
Other investment	1,260	1,260	1,260	1,260	1,260	1,260	1,260	1,260	1,260	1,260	1,260
Direct operating	1,975	1,385	1,435	1,485	1,535	1,485	1,480	1,335	1,165	920	1,420
Indirect operating	2,015	1,660	1,690	1,720	1,750	1,720	1,720	1,630	1,530	1,380	1,682
Total	5,300	5,265	6,605	6,945	6,550	6,720	7,590	7,455	4,510	3,810	6,076

a. Bombers and missile carriers are based on ninety interior bases.

We also assumed that 40 percent of the indirect costs for the bomber force were fixed and would not vary with changes in the structure of the force. The Department of Defense estimated that 37 percent of the support manpower to operate bases, which constitutes a significant part of indirect operating costs, was fixed in fiscal 1973.[1] The remaining 60 percent of the indirect operating costs were considered to vary directly with changes in direct operating costs for the various alternatives.

Tables A-4 through A-8 show in greater detail the force projections and costs of the alternative postures compared in chapter 6.

1. U.S. Department of Defense, "Military Manpower Requirements Report for FY 1973" (February 1972; processed), p. 79.

The Mathematics of Prelaunch Survivability (Ground Alert)

The problem of bomber survivability starts with the launch of the attacking missiles. In our calculations, time is set to zero at the instant the attacking missiles are launched. After this launch there is a delay before the bombers can begin to take off. This delay—from the instant that missiles are launched to the instant that bomber brakes are released—is defined in this analysis as bomber reaction time, which is treated as an independent variable. Once the takeoff begins, the location of the bombers becomes uncertain. The area of uncertainty increases as the bombers pick up speed and fly farther from their bases; it is centered on the point at which each aircraft reaches a safe speed to turn, since before that point is reached the location of the bomber is highly predictable. The time used by the bomber to accelerate to safe turning speed is added to the bomber reaction time as defined here. In practice, it matters very little whether the area of uncertainty is assumed to be centered on the takeoff point (with the time for takeoff included in the bomber flyout profile) or on the point at which safe turning speed is attained (with the time for takeoff included in bomber reaction time). Because we lacked data on the speeds at which various aircraft reach safe turning speed, we centered the area of uncertainty on the takeoff point.

The flight time of the missiles depends on the distance they must fly and the type of trajectory used. The flight times of submarine-launched ballistic missiles (SLBMs) might vary from about seven minutes to fifteen minutes or more.[1]

1. Overpressure and dynamic pressure propagate from a nuclear explosion at about the speed of sound, about 1,130 feet per second at sea level. Thermal effects, electromagnetic pulse effects, and radioactivity propagate at the speed of light (186,000 miles per second). For aircraft vulnerable to overpressure or dynamic pressure, the propagation time, in effect, adds to the flight time of the missile, a period equal to the lethal radius for the weapon and aircraft in question divided by the

Table B-1. **Lethal Radii against Targets of Varying Hardness for 1- and 2-Megaton Warheads**

	Lethal radius (feet)	
Target hardness (pounds per square inch)	1-megaton yield	2-megaton yield
1	55,000	70,000
2	42,000	53,000
3	34,400	43,500
4	25,300	32,000
5	21,800	27,400
6	19,000	24,000

The area of uncertainty, A_u, at the time the attacking missiles arrive is given by

$$(1) \qquad A_u = \pi R_u^2$$

where R_u is the distance the bomber flies as a function of time after brake release; R_u depends on bomber flyout characteristics and on the difference between the time of flight of the missiles and bomber reaction time.

The warhead on each reliable attacking missile will create a lethal area that depends on the hardness of the aircraft and on the warhead yield. Table B-1 shows lethal radii as a function of airplane hardness and warhead yield; weapons are assumed to be detonated at optimum altitude.

The lethal area, A_L, of each warhead is given by:

$$(2) \qquad A_L = \pi R_L^2$$

where R_L is the lethal radius.

The probability that a warhead destroys a bomber, P_d, is then given by:

$$(3) \qquad P_d = r_m (R_L / R_u)^2, \quad \text{for } R_L \leqq R_u,$$

where r_m is the reliability of the attacking missile (assumed to be 85 percent in this study).

The probability of survival, P_s, is thus

$$(4) \qquad P_s = 1 - r_m (R_L / R_u)^2.$$

speed of sound. For hard airplanes—3 to 6 psi—and 1-megaton weapons, this would amount to fifteen to thirty seconds; for soft airplanes—1 to 2 psi—forty to fifty seconds. The use of several small weapons instead of one large one would reduce propagation time. Moreover, if the aircraft are vulnerable to thermal effects (and overpressure is merely a surrogate specification of hardness), propagation time would be essentially zero. Throughout this study we have assumed a propagation time of zero.

Bomber bases might be attacked by a barrage of several missiles. We assumed that the attacker would know the area of uncertainty that must be barraged and would target his weapons in it to maximize the portion of the area covered by lethal weapon effects.

If warheads arrived simultaneously or within a few seconds of each other in the vicinity of an air base, for maximum effect they would be targeted so that each covered a separate portion of the area of uncertainty. If the intervals between weapons lasted for many seconds, say thirty, time would be available between weapon arrivals for an aircraft to fly into an area covered by earlier weapons. Thus it would be less important for weapons to be targeted to cover virgin portions of the area of uncertainty. In this analysis, we assume essentially simultaneous arrival of attacking weapons.

For certain combinations of lethal radius, radius of uncertainty, and weapon numbers, the lethal areas will overlap. For two weapons, overlap begins when the lethal radius is half the radius of uncertainty. For three weapons, overlap begins when the lethal radius is about 46 percent of the radius of uncertainty. From equation (4), the survival probability at which overlap occurs for three weapons is about 50 percent. It can be shown on a case-by-case basis that for larger numbers of weapons overlap will not occur at survival probabilities greater than about 50 percent. Thus for two or more weapons

$$(5) \qquad P_s = 1 - nr_m(R_L/R_u)^2, \quad \text{for } P_s \geq 0.5,$$

where n = the number of missiles assigned a given bomber base.

When P_s is less than 50 percent, the geometry of the overlapping lethal areas must be taken into account. This has been done in calculations presented in this paper for values of n of four or less. When n is greater than four, extrapolations between P_s of 50 percent and 30 percent have been used. Values below 30 percent are of little or no interest in a study of this sort.

Figure B-1 presents survival probability as a function of R_L/R_u for various values of n. To use the figure, the reader should divide the number of SLBMs in the attack by the number of bomber bases (bombers are assumed to be distributed equally over the bases) to get n; then subtract the bomber reaction time from the SLBM flight time. The difference between the two times can be used to determine the radius of uncertainty from figure 4-1; taking the appropriate lethal radius from table B-1 allows a computation of R_L/R_u. This value and the value of n previously cal-

Figure B-1. Bomber Survival Probability versus the Ratio of Lethal Radius to the Radius of Uncertainty for Various Levels of Attack[a]

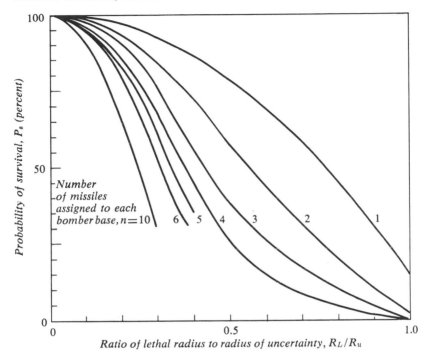

a. SLBM reliability is 85 percent.

culated can be used to determine the value of bomber survivability from figure B-1. The reader must keep in mind the following key assumptions underlying these curves in order to judge the appropriateness of the results:

—All bombers take off simultaneously.

—All SLBMs arrive simultaneously.

—SLBM reliability is assumed to be 85 percent.

Air Defense Penetration Calculations

In chapter 5 we described how well high-performance area defenses might work under limiting assumptions about their effectiveness. These area defenses were approximated by a simple "subtractive," or "exhaustion," model. Using this model, we estimated the number of SRAMs a bomber force will deliver as follows:[1]

$$(1) \qquad S = B(n - d)r_b r_m \left(\frac{Bdr_b r_m + Br_b - I}{Bdr_b r_m + Br_b} \right),$$

where

$S =$ number of reliable SRAMs delivered,
$n =$ number of SRAM and decoy spaces per bomber,
$d =$ number of decoys per bomber,
$B =$ number of alert surviving bombers,
$r_b =$ reliability of the bombers,
$r_m =$ reliability of missiles (SRAMs or decoys),
$I =$ number of intercepts the defense can enforce.

If equation (1) is solved for B, differentiated with respect to d, the derivative of B with respect to d set equal to zero and the resulting equation solved for d, an expression for the decoy loading per bomber that will minimize the number of bombers needed to deliver a specified number of reliable SRAMs is obtained:

$$(2) \qquad d^* = \frac{n - (1/r_m)\sqrt{S/I}}{\sqrt{S/I} + 1},$$

1. The model is called a subtractive model because the number of intercepts, I, the defense can enforce are subtracted from the number of penetrators (see the numerator of the bracketed fraction in equation [1]). Equation (1) is sometimes called an exhaustion model because the intercepts, I, must be "exhausted" before any bomber or decoys can penetrate.

112

where d^* is the particular value of d that minimizes B. Then B^*, the minimum size bomber force needed to deliver S SRAMs, is

$$(3) \qquad B^* = \frac{1}{r_m r_b} \left[\frac{S}{n - d^*} + \frac{I}{d^* + (1/r_m)} \right].$$

Should the air defense system be able to identify which penetrators are bombers and which are decoys and be able to attack the bombers preferentially, the number of decoys that will penetrate the area defenses, D', can be obtained as follows for $I \geqq Br_b$:

$$(4) \qquad D' = r_m r_b Bd^* + Br_b - I.$$

The reason for arming the decoys is apparent from these considerations. If the decoys were not armed, and if $I \geq Br_b$, no lethal payload would penetrate. If the decoys were armed, however, D' decoys would get through and do some damage. Moreover, if Soviet air defense controllers knew the decoys were armed, they would have an incentive to attack them, even if the decoys were identified as such.

These equations were used to calculate tables 5-1 and 5-2 and to determine the sizes of the penetrating forces described in chapter 6.

Cruise missile force calculations were made with the following equation:

$$(5) \qquad B = (C + I)/nr_b r_m,$$

where C is the number of reliable cruise missiles to be delivered and n is the number of cruise missiles per bomber. This equation was used to calculate table 5-3. The quantity $(C + I)/r_b r_m$ is the total number of cruise missiles that must be in the force to ensure delivery of C missiles; dividing this quantity by n, the number of missiles per carrier yields B, the number of aircraft required. All reliabilities were taken to be 90 percent in these calculations.

In chapter 5 we also presented estimates of the number of SAM batteries that would have to be suppressed to permit unimpeded cruise missile attacks on defended cities. Those estimates were made in the following way:

First, the number of SAMs deployed at each city was determined by setting the density of SAMs along the defended perimeter at each city proportional to the respective population of each city (the surrogate for the value of the city). We imposed this rule so that each "unit" of SAM site suppression effort would, on the average, expose the same number of people to cruise missile attack. The total number of SAM batteries was of course constrained to the threat level under study. Thus

(6) $$d_i = kp_i$$

where d_i = number of SAMs per unit of defended perimeter at the ith city,

p_i = population in the ith city,

k = constant of proportionality (evaluated by equation [10]).

Then,

(7) $$n_i = d_i c_i,$$

where n_i = number of SAM sites at ith city,

c_i = defended perimeter of the ith city.

Hence,

(8) $$n_i = kp_i c_i$$

and

(9) $$\sum_{i=1}^{50} n_i = k \sum_{i=1}^{50} p_i c_i.$$

Let N = the total number of SAM sites deployed at the fifty largest cities. Then

$$N = \sum_{i=1}^{50} n_i$$

and, from equation (9),

(10) $$k = N / \sum_{i=1}^{50} p_i c_i.$$

Also,

(11) $$d_i = Np_i / \sum_{i=1}^{50} p_i c_i$$

$$= Np_i / 2\pi \Sigma p_i R_i,$$

where R_i = radius of the defended perimeter.

All SAM sites that would have to be destroyed to permit cruise missile penetration would be within one SAM site lethal radius of the axis of cruise missile attack. Thus

(12) $$S_i = 2d_i R_L,$$

Table C-1. Fifty Largest Soviet Cities, Their Populations, and the Radius of the Circle Enclosing 95 Percent of the Built-up Area of Each City

City	Population (millions)	Radius of circle enclosing 95 percent of the population (nautical miles)	City	Population (millions)	Radius of circle enclosing 95 percent of the population (nautical miles)
1. Moscow	9.1	8.4	26. Minsk	0.75	4.7
2. Leningrad	4.0	5.2	27. Zaporozhe	0.75	4.5
3. Kharkov	1.5	4.8	28. Krivoy-Rog	0.70	3.4
4. Baku	1.4	3.4	29. Lvov	0.69	3.2
5. Kiev	1.4	3.8	30. Alma-Ata	0.67	4.1
6. Novosibirsk	1.3	6.6	31. Yaroslavl	0.66	3.0
7. Gorki	1.3	8.8	32. Novokuznetsk	0.57	2.9
8. Tashkent	1.1	3.8	33. Makeevka	0.56	2.2
9. Donetsk	1.1	2.7	34. Zhdanov	0.54	2.9
10. Kuybyshev	1.1	3.0	35. Krasnoyarsk	0.54	4.6
11. Sverdlovsk	1.1	6.2	36. Krasnodar	0.53	3.5
12. Dnepropetrovsk	1.0	4.5	37. Karaganda	0.52	5.2
13. Odessa	1.0	5.0	38. Tula	0.51	2.8
14. Tiflis	1.0	3.9	39. Irkutsk	0.51	2.6
15. Rostov-Na-Donu	0.99	3.7	40. Gorlovka	0.49	4.0
16. Kazan	0.95	5.0	41. Barnaul	0.48	2.9
17. Chelyabinsk	0.94	3.7	42. Kharbarovsk	0.47	5.6
18. Perm	0.89	5.5	43. Lugansk	0.46	2.2
19. Volgograd	0.82	7.9	44. Ivanovo	0.45	4.6
20. Voronezh	0.80	3.0	45. Vladivostok	0.45	3.1
21. Saratov	0.79	4.1	46. Nizhni Tagil	0.45	4.0
22. Yerevan	0.78	3.5	47. Kemerovo	0.44	3.0
23. Ufa	0.78	2.6	48. Kalinin	0.42	3.0
24. Riga	0.77	4.9	49. Magnitogorsk	0.42	3.2
25. Omsk	0.77	4.4	50. Frunze	0.41	2.4

Source: Derived from *Narodnoye Khozyaistvo SSSR, v. 1963 g* (Moscow: Central'noye Statisticheskoye, 1965) and furnished to the authors by Ricardo de Sobrino.

where S_i = number of SAM sites that must be destroyed,
    R_L = SAM site lethal radius.

Hence,

$$S_i = Np_i R_L / \pi \Sigma p_i R_i, \quad \text{for } S_i \leq 0.5\, n_i;$$

and
$$S_i = 0.5\, n_i, \quad \text{for } S_i \geq 0.5\, n_i.$$

The constraint that S_i not exceed $0.5\, n_i$ was imposed on the ground that SAMs are unlikely to be able to attack low-altitude targets approaching from behind the SAM site—that is, approaching from more than 90 degrees in azimuth from the axis of the SAM's primary field of fire.

The estimates in tables 5-4 and 5-5 were based on the data in table C-1, where R_i was taken to be 1.5 times the radius enclosing 95 percent of the built-up areas of the fifty largest cities.